CHINA'S PEACEFUL RISE

SPEECHES OF
ZHENG BIJIAN

1997–2005

BROOKINGS INSTITUTION PRESS
Washington, D.C.

Copyright © 2005
THE BROOKINGS INSTITUTION
1775 Massachusetts Avenue, N.W., Washington, D.C. 20036
www.brookings.edu

Library of Congress Cataloging-in-Publication data are available.
ISBN-13: 978-0-8157-9725-8
ISBN-10: 0-8157-9725-7

9 8 7 6 5 4 3 2 1

The paper used in this publication meets minimum requirements of the American National Standard for Information Sciences—Permanence of Paper for Printed Library Materials: ANSI Z39.48-1992.

CHINA'S PEACEFUL RISE

Contents

FOREWORD

In the more than two decades since Deng Xiaoping began China's process of opening and reform, Zheng Bijian has been one of China's leading thinkers and writers on ideological questions. From a variety of senior Communist Party positions, ranging from scholarly work at the Central Party School of China to high management positions at the Propaganda Department, he has brought his intellectual energy to some of the most difficult questions that China has confronted. Zheng is now chairman of the China Reform Forum, a Beijing-based think tank working on domestic and international issues. Some of his most important recent work has been gathered here for the first time in English. Most of it is devoted to the idea of China's "peaceful rise," a concept that Zheng has advocated and with which he is strongly identified. Following release of this volume, the Brookings Institution's China Initiative intends periodically to publish for English-speaking audiences additional writings by other important Chinese thinkers in the fields of politics, economics, and society.

In 1992 Zheng became executive vice president of the Central Party School, serving as deputy to Chinese President Hu Jintao. In that role, Zheng worked closely with Hu to overhaul the school and turn it into a center for educating the next generation of Chinese leaders. As a result, he enjoys a distinctive relationship with some of the leading figures in China today, representing a link between the reform thinking of Deng's time and the contemporary development challenges of China. When Zheng reached retirement age in 2002, he set aside his work at the Party School and moved to the China Reform Forum, which he has used as a platform for research and strategic thinking about China's position in the world.

The questions Zheng seeks to address in the peaceful rise speeches collected here include some of the most complex issues China faces as it emerges into an already rapidly changing world order. Originally conceived in 2002, as an attempt to answer Western proponents of the "China threat" theory, Zheng's idea of a peaceful rise now includes views on China's internal situation as well. The works in this volume show Zheng attempting to explain the strategic background of China's peaceful rise, to demonstrate how this rise can be accomplished, and to address clearly the challenges to a peaceful rise. The message Zheng brings is, first and foremost, that China hopes to rise not through territorial expansion or challenges to other powers but as a result of its own hard work and a peaceful international environment. Unlike earlier rising powers, which upset the international order either to facilitate their rise or as a result of it, Zheng says China seeks a different path and will work to integrate itself into the world order instead of challenging it. This demands a continued effort by China to seek and support interdependency, a development path that will also lead China to seek cooperative economic and security relationships.

Zheng's concept of a peaceful rise doesn't depend on China alone, as critics inside China have been quick to point out. It also demands that the rest of the world help China create an international environment where this sort of rise can take place. And it demands that China quickly deal with the internal problems facing a peaceful rise. Zheng seeks to address these issues in his later speeches, which refine his core idea. The internal challenges to a peaceful rise are many, Zheng asserts. These include resource shortages, pollution, corruption, the need for a rule of law, and uneven socioeconomic development. Internationally, China faces a host of established powers—most notably the United States— with their own economic and political concerns. Zheng believes that clearly explaining China's intentions can help establish the basis of a larger cooperative framework that will smooth China's growth in economic and political influence. It will also provide a guiding principle for Chinese leaders and citizens as they look for solutions to complex problems. There are countervailing schools of thought in China, some of them quite influential. Zheng's initial discussion of peaceful rise was met by opposition from some influential minds in China. Some argued the theory's focus on peace made China look weak, while others argued that the idea was too simplistic for a complex world. Yet another criticism was that Zheng's theory was naive, since the United States and other established powers won't, in these critics' view, permit China to rise at all, let alone peacefully. For many observers of China, however, this energetic debate about grand strategy was in itself promising, proof of increasing openness in discussion about what direction the country should look toward for its future as a global power.

As a result, this collection of Zheng's work gives not only a view of one possible Chinese future but also a glimpse into how Chinese thinkers are, at this moment, debating their future. Zheng's view of a peaceful rise for China is a Chinese grand strategy that we know is well regarded in certain circles in Beijing. In recent months, Zheng has been reminding listeners that a peaceful rise can be seen as an extension of Deng's often-stated idea of "peace and development." What emerges most strongly from the speeches here is Zheng's firm sense that the lessons of history demand that China pursue a stable, peaceful international environment as a first priority. In Zheng's view, that sort of peace-based grand strategy will not only help smooth China's rise—it will also make it easier to see that China's success translates into benefits for other countries as well.

The speeches in this volume are worth reading not only for the strength of their ideas, but to begin building a picture of the political and policy constraints and opportunities in relations with China. The breadth of Zheng's ideas allows him to tackle subjects as diverse as energy security and nuclear proliferation, always with a strong focus on the costs to China of a rise that is not peaceful. Zheng leaves us to calculate for ourselves the related costs to the rest of the world. It is a theme that informs all of these speeches and helps us better answer this key question for America: How should we think about China?

JOHN L. THORNTON
Chair of the Board, Brookings Institution
July 2005

CHINA'S PEACEFUL RISE

China's New Road of Peaceful Rise and Chinese-U.S. Relations

Brookings Institution, June 16, 2005

It is a great pleasure for me to visit Washington again and come to the Brookings Institution, an important U.S. think tank, to exchange views with you. I hope that our dialogue will lead to better mutual understanding, more common ground, greater mutual trust, and less misgiving in the interest of more positive and stable relations between China and the United States.

I know there has been heated discussion in recent years in U.S. political circles, major think tanks, and the media on whether or not China's peaceful rise will threaten America's global interests. Some important, constructive, enlightening, and interesting viewpoints have been presented. I hope my speech will contribute to the discussion. However, let me assure you that I am not here to debate with you. I just want to talk about solid facts, rather than abstract concepts, in the following ten points.

First, what has happened in the past two decades and more shows that China's peaceful rise is not a threat but an opportunity for the United States. Since China began to pursue a policy of reform and opening up in the late 1970s, it has opted to seek a peaceful international environment for development and, by its own development, contribute to the maintenance of world peace. China's peaceful rise can be understood as both a road and a goal of national development. As a road to development, it means China will independently build socialism with Chinese characteristics, by integrating with and not divorcing itself from economic globalization, and pursuing mutually beneficial relations with other countries. As a goal of development, it means China will realize basic modernization by the mid-twenty-first century, overcome its underdevelopment and catch up with medium-level developed countries. By integrating China's modernization drive with economic globalization, we mean that China will take an active part in economic globalization and will not change the international order and configuration through violence. Independently building socialism with Chinese characteristics means we will mainly rely on our own effort to solve our problems, without causing trouble to others. The experience of the past two decades has demonstrated that this road of peaceful rise works. In this process, while China has been becoming stronger, the United States has maintained robust growth. Common development and mutually beneficial results have been achieved for both countries. Sino-U.S. cooperation has expanded from the political field to all dimensions, including economic, cultural, military, and security.

Second, along with the deepening of our bilateral relations, American understanding of China's peaceful rise is gradually deepening. Of late, I have found quite a few impartial and positive comments or reports about China's peaceful rise by some influential media sources such as the *New York Times*, the *International Herald Tribune*, the *Asian Wall Street Journal*, and *Newsweek*. In addition, the well-known journal *Foreign Affairs* has in recent years published weighty analytical articles about China's peaceful rise. I am also delighted to hear a growing voice on Capitol Hill calling for closer Chinese-U.S. relations, in particular, the bill cosponsored by two senators on increasing cul-

tural exchanges. A special mention must be made of President
Bush's answers to questions about China, which I find quite positive. He has said that China's rise is "an amazing story"; China is
a "massive market," an "economic opportunity," and a security
"partner"; "the relationship with China is a very complex one"
and a simplistic approach should be avoided. Furthermore, President Bush has rejected calls from Capitol Hill for sanctions
against China under Section 301 of U.S. trade law provisions on
the pretext of the RMB exchange rate. All this shows that more
and more thoughtful people from both political parties and various circles in the United States are beginning to face up to the
reality of a peacefully rising China and to think about how to deal
with it. It is a new and encouraging sign.

Third, the Chinese leadership is soberly aware of existing and
future problems. The peaceful rise of a country with a population
of 1.3 billion to 1.5 billion is by no means an easy task. This is
especially true in the first half of the twenty-first century, when
China is faced with both a "golden period of development" and
an "intense period of paradoxes." There are three fundamental
challenges in this regard. The first is resources, especially energy.
The second is the environment. The third is a series of paradoxes
in the process of economic and social development, such as
uneven development between the coastal areas and the hinter-
land, the contradiction between fairness and economic returns,
rural-urban disparity, the wealth gap, and the tension between
reform and stability. If these three challenges cannot be settled
satisfactorily, then not only will your worries remain, but China's
peaceful rise will also be extremely difficult.

Fourth, China has already formulated three strategies to cope
with the three challenges. This is of vital importance. The first

3

strategy is to transcend the old-style industrialization and opt for a new style. We will never take on the old-style industrialization, characterized by high input, high consumption, and high pollution. Instead, China will blaze a new road of industrialization, featuring high technology input, economic efficiency, low consumption of resources, and low pollution and giving full play to its strength in human resources. The second strategy is to transcend the traditional development approaches that big powers have taken in modern history and the cold war mentality marked by ideology, and to take an active part in economic globalization. This is because China's peaceful rise benefits from economic globalization, which in turn facilitates the achievement of this goal. The third strategy is to transcend outdated forms of social management and continue to build a harmonious socialist society. It is necessary to build a social network that links government control mechanisms with social coordination mechanisms, complement government administrative functions with social self-regulating functions, and fuse government management forces with forces for social change with a view to improving governance and social management. These three strategies can be summed up as maintaining external peace and internal harmony, which are interconnected and complementary, and leading the 1.3 billion to 1.5 billion Chinese people toward a better life and greater contribution to humanity in the context of mutually beneficial cooperation with other countries. Therefore, China's peaceful rise is the ascent of a staunch force defending rather than disrupting global peace. It is by no means a peril. It is a blessing for the world.

Fifth, these three strategies and China's development path of peaceful rise share a distinct feature: resolving our problems on our own. This is what we mean by Chinese characteristics and the coherence of China's foreign and domestic policies. That is to say, we link our peaceful rise with the social reform and transformation within the country and focus on building a Chinese-style socialist society that is modern and harmonious. Such a society has several dimensions. First, it is a resource-efficient society with Chinese characteristics. We address the thorny problem of shortages of energy and other resources by implementing the policy of depending on domestic resources, giving priority to energy saving, improving the energy structure, and appropriately developing cooperation with foreign countries. The past twenty years has seen China quadruple its GDP at the cost of doubling its energy consumption. In the next twenty years, China is set to quadruple its GDP again, by doubling its energy consumption. That is to say, China has to adopt various ways to remain no less than 90 percent self-sufficient in energy for the twenty years to come, and embark on a Chinese-style path of energy saving and environmentally friendly sustainable development. Second, it features urbanization with Chinese characteristics. China has a workforce of 750 million, 500 million of whom are in the countryside. In the first twenty years of this century, 200 million more unemployed and underemployed rural workers will join those who have already come to work in the city. Migration on such a vast scale is unprecedented in world history. Third, it is a live-and-learn society with Chinese characteristics. To press ahead with China's urbanization process at a reasonable pace, we must strengthen employment training for the rural population, young people in particular, and build a live-and-learn society. Fourth, it is a society of coordinated regional development with Chinese characteristics. For the next twenty years, clusters of cities around the Pearl River Delta, the Yangtze River Delta, and the Bohai Sea Rim will continue to be the engine of China's development. At the same time, China will continue to implement a set of policies to rejuvenate the northeast, and develop the central and western part of the country, and gradually realize coordinated development among different regions.

Sixth, China's peaceful rise is a "Chinese dream." In energy consumption, for example, we can't afford an "American dream." The per capita oil consumption of the United States is currently 25 barrels a year, while the figure for China stands at less than 1.5 barrels. If the Chinese come close to the current U.S. level of oil consumption in the twenty-first century, how much would our energy consumption grow—ten-, twenty-, a hundredfold? This is dreadful to contemplate, both for China and for the whole world. And in population flow, we will not pursue the "European dream" either. Europe rose by sending more than 60 million people overseas to set up colonies. This might have been a rosy dream for some Europeans at that time. However, it was a nightmare for all those who were subjected to their colonial rule. We Chinese have to rely on our own efforts to address the migration problem within our own territory. And, in the enhancement of our national strength, we do not want to dream a "Soviet Union dream." If you compare China's social reform and national transformation in the process of its peaceful rise in the first half of the twenty-first century with the Soviet Union's arms race, expansionism, and hegemony under President Brezhnev and its so-called world revolution and export of revolution, you will find nothing in common.

Seventh, by following a development path of peaceful rise, we are not seeking to become a big military power contending for

hegemony around the world, but a big market, a major civilization, and a responsible big power playing a constructive role in
the international community. Speaking of a big market, China
was considered the "biggest potential market" twenty years ago.
Today, China's huge market potential is being turned into a reality. China has, since the Asian financial crisis in 1997 in particular, contributed a lot to the trade and GDP growth of the whole
world. A decade ago, some of the world's top telecommunication
companies, such as Motorola, were just beginning to do business
in China; today, the number of mobile phone subscribers in my
country has reached 340 million, more than a quarter of China's
total population. Now, most of the world's top 500 companies
have entered the Chinese market, as have many well-known
American companies. Of the top ten foreign companies export-
ing from China in 2004, three are American. In 2004, 24.3 percent of exports by foreign companies in China went to the United
States. If the United States opens itself up as a tourist destination
to Chinese citizens, like many Southeast Asian countries, the
huge number of Chinese tourists will further contribute to
American economic growth. By building a major civilization, we
mean China's rise will boost the calibre of the Chinese nation and
realize the great renaissance of its culture. To quote Lee Kwan
Yew, minister mentor of Singapore, "China's ambition is not to
conquer the world, but to rekindle its civilization with vibrant,
high, and popular culture." In short, by unswerving adherence to
a development path of peaceful rise, we seek to become a modern
socialist country that is prosperous, democratic, and culturally
advanced, and a responsible big country playing a constructive
role in international affairs, which neither seeks hegemony or
leadership of the world nor becomes a vassal state.

Eighth, since the goal of the Chinese Communist Party (CCP) and China's development path is peaceful rise, as mentioned before, what is there for the United States to worry about? Former EU Commission president Romano Prodi recently said at the Bo'ao Forum for Asia held in China that we don't need economists to tell us when China will become the world's first or second manufacturer or exporter. What we want to know is what values China will adopt. I agree with him. To understand whether China's peaceful rise will threaten America's global interests, Americans have first to understand the new concepts of the Chinese leadership since the Third Plenum of the Eleventh Party Congress.

On this issue, I would respectfully draw your attention to the following five key points. First, in his late years, Deng Xiaoping said, "China does not seek hegemony now, neither will it do so even if it becomes stronger, and we must let our future generations remember this." This was his political testament. Time and again, he stressed that China must stick to the policy of reform and opening up for a long time and adhere to this basic guideline for 100 years to come. Second, Jiang Zemin put forward the important concept of the "three represents," which carries on Deng Xiaoping's theory. Jiang places greater emphasis on economic globalization, which he thinks is an irreversible trend of the times, and China's participation in it. He also points out that the world is colorful; China must develop its culture while learning from the achievements of all of human civilization. Third, the new Chinese leadership with Hu Jintao as general secretary of the CCP, further emancipating the mind and advocating pragmatism and keeping abreast with the changing times, is pursuing a foreign policy of peace, a domestic policy of building a harmo-

nious society, and the basic concept of reconciliation with Taiwan. These ideas have already exerted and will continue to have
a vital impact on China's domestic and foreign affairs. Fourth,
the realization of the country's peaceful rise by the mid-twenty-
first century will keep our leadership and several generations of
the Chinese people very busy. We must concentrate all our energy
on fulfilling this task. We have neither the intention of threatening others nor the energy to do so. Fifth, China is the beneficiary
of the current international order, particularly economic globalization. China stands for reform, rather than violence, in the
efforts to establish a new international political and economic
order. If people fail to see these important and basic concepts of
the Chinese leadership, which are in conformity with the trends
of our times, they may arrive at a serious strategic misjudgment
of China's direction in the twenty-first century.

Ninth, change your mind-set, outlook, and perspective and
you would realize that intrinsic opportunities abound in across-
the-board exchanges and cooperation between China and the
United States and that the Sino-U.S. relations enjoy a bright
future. I said here two years ago that it was wrong to characterize
the Chinese-U.S. relationship as driven by external forces. This
line of thinking suggests that the "polar bear," which disappeared
after the end of the cold war and the era of world hegemony, and
bin Laden, who orchestrated the September 11 attacks, were the
glue of the Chinese-U.S. relationship; that the relationship would
go wrong once the polar bear or the terrorist threat was removed.
Wouldn't it be too pathetic to place our hope for a better relationship totally on the motivation of external forces? Some have
suggested that an emerging power will inevitably pursue a hawk-
ish foreign policy, wage a protracted cold war, and harm others

for selfish gain. This, in my opinion, is an outdated view, based on old-fashioned theories. I appreciate the views expressed by my old friend Zbigniew Brzezinski at a recent Carnegie Foundation discussion on China's peaceful rise. He said, in effect, that if a theory is proven incompatible with the real world, that theory should be corrected. I also agree with what Richard Haass, who used to be at Brookings, said: that China only exports computers, not revolution or ideology. These sober observations deserve acknowledgement because they are based on fact and not on rigid doctrines. In my view, both now and in the future, Chinese-U.S. relations have great opportunities and the two countries have a broad horizon for parallel development.

The first opportunity for relations between China and the United States comes from a high degree of convergence of their national interests and mutual needs in the age of globalization. This explains the phenomenal growth of two-way trade, from some U.S. $500 million at the end of the 1970s to the current U.S. $170 billion, and the fact that China is spending more than 70 percent of its U.S. $660 billion foreign exchange reserves on U.S. Treasury bonds. Thus, the two countries have had so many common interests that it is very difficult to unravel their relationship. That is why any friction between them over trade will not easily become emotionally charged or politicized. If the United States can handle such trade disputes in an "apolitical" way, Chinese-U.S. trade ties will surely make a big leap forward, instead of a big step backward.

The second opportunity for Chinese-U.S. relations comes from the new security concept of "major-country cooperation," in response to increased nontraditional security threats. I agree with an often-repeated view of President Bush and Secretary of

State Condoleezza Rice that in today's world, a war between major countries would be unthinkable. Now, faced with a common and ferocious enemy in terrorism, the proliferation of weapons of mass destruction, and other nontraditional security threats, we have every reason to deepen cooperation in the area of strategic security. The key is to have mutual trust at the strategic level. I want to stress here that respecting history and taking account of the reality, China holds a pragmatic attitude toward the American presence, including its military presence, in the Asia-Pacific region, and takes a position of "open multilateralism" with respect to Asia-Pacific integration propelled by an East Asia community. The argument that China is pushing for the United States to be ostracized from the Asia-Pacific region is groundless fabrication, designed only to sow discord between the two countries.

The third opportunity for relations between the United States and China comes from their interest in settling regional hot spots and their joint efforts to maintain international order. The Asia-Pacific provides the stage for the common development of China and the United States. Yet this is an unsettled region that has witnessed both the cold war and hot wars. It falls on our two countries to remove the lingering legacy of the cold war and rise to the real challenges of averting hot wars. If China and the United States can look at the various issues from such a commanding height, it is possible for them to stay clear of the type of interference noted above—"China is pursuing an Asian version of the Monroe Doctrine to push out the Americans"—work closely together to defuse existing conflicts, and plan for a future that features peace, coexistence, and common development on the basis of the mutual accommodation of their respective interests.

Furthermore, China and the United States share the duty and obligation to maintain a stable international order and work out its proper reform. We should open our minds and work together to explore new global economic, financial, political, and security mechanisms.

The fourth opportunity for Chinese-U.S. relations comes from the coexistence of and interaction between our two civilizations. Globalization, in our view, is not the "clash of civilizations." Rather, it is a time of intercultural exchanges and harmony between civilizations. Cultural exchanges and cooperation with the United States have already become an important part of an emerging Chinese cultural and media market. A thorough understanding of Chinese culture has increasingly become a crucial condition for the United States to live harmoniously with China. I have been told that a gubernatorial candidate in Utah made a campaign promise that if elected, he would introduce Chinese language courses in every public school. The growing craze for the Chinese language and Chinese culture in the United States, and the senators' bill to strengthen cultural exchanges with China that I mentioned above, will usher in an unprecedented new period of Sino-American cultural exchange in the first half of the twenty-first century. Currently, our interaction through education, culture, science, and technology is going strong; our cooperation over the Olympic Games and AIDS prevention is full of vigor; and the two sides are working together to act quickly on a travel agreement for Chinese tourists in the United States. The future for Chinese-U.S. cultural cooperation is indeed very bright.

Tenth, I would also like to point out that we can't just wait passively for opportunities to come to our doorstep. We should roll up our sleeves and create them. Not long ago, a former American official said the following to me: If China and the United States can work in closer cooperation, then the twenty-first century will be a great century. But if the relationship moves back, the twenty-first century will be a very bad one for the two countries and the world. I could not agree more. It takes two hands to make a clap, so fresh headway in Chinese-U.S. relations calls for common efforts by both governments. Let me suggest to my American friends, when you look at China's rise and Chinese-U.S. relations, you may perhaps need to rise above three things: The first is cold war thinking, which follows ideological lines and positions one according to social systems. When someone subscribes to such thinking, he is very likely to make a strategic misjudgment about Chinese-style socialism and the Chinese Communist Party. The second is the sense of cultural superiority that takes one's own values as the yardstick of right and wrong. Today, after all, we already live in a brand new age, with many civilizations living side by side and different cultures interacting productively. The third thing that should be overcome is the traditional theory that the emerging power is bound to challenge the existing dominant power; this theory cannot explain China's peaceful rise and the fact that rising China is a staunch force for world peace.

In conclusion, please allow me to quote two great Chinese leaders. Mao Zedong, the founder of New China, said in the 1950s, "China will become a great, strong, and also friendly country." Deng Xiaoping, the chief architect of China's program of reform and opening, said in the 1980s, "Relations between China and the United States must eventually be improved." Let me present the words of these two wise men to my American friends here, hoping you will agree with them and tell your friends and colleagues about them. I also hope that you will be disposed to embrace China's peaceful rise.

13

A New Path for China's Peaceful Rise and the Future of Asia

Bo'ao Forum for Asia, 2003

I would like briefly to share my observations on the following topics: how to view China's development; how to view the path of China's rise; and how to view the relationship between China's rise and Asia.

It has been precisely a quarter of a century since the inception of China's reform and opening up. During these twenty-five years, China has made important progress and scored a series of new achievements. It started to become a well-off society at the beginning of the twenty-first century, and is now concentrating on building on that achievement for the benefit of the whole economy.

However, we are soberly aware that at present economic development is not comprehensive, it is unequal, and it remains at a low level. There is still a long way to go. China remains a developing country, and a developing country facing a host of big problems at that.

So, what are these big problems? Here are two simple mathematical propositions. One concerns multiplication, the other concerns division:

—Multiplied by 1.3 billion, any problem of economic or social development, no matter how small and negligible it seems to be, will become a big or even a huge problem.

—Divided by 1.3 billion, China's financial and material

resources, no matter how abundant they are, will be at extremely low per capita levels.

It must be quite clear that this 1.3 billion refers to China's large population. And this is not yet its peak. Our population will not start to drop until 2030, after it has reached 1.5 billion.

Of course, one should not lose sight of the other side of the coin. China's experience of reform and opening up during the past twenty-five years has demonstrated the magnitude of its labor force, its creativity, its purchasing power, the cohesion and momentum of development, and its contribution to the world as an engine of growth. Once all the positive factors in China are fully mobilized and its economy is revived, it looks like there will be another mathematical proposition related to the number 1.3 billion or 1.5 billion.

Thus, in the final analysis, China's development and rise—both the negative and the positive aspects—are inseparable from the number 1.3 billion or 1.5 billion. In this context, all our attempts to solve our development problems, whether concerning economic, political, or cultural affairs, and whether in terms of domestic, foreign, or defense policy, have been for the purpose of securing a comfortable life for China's 1.3 billion, or even 1.5 billion, people. We will never slacken our efforts to bring about a better, richer, more decent, and more humane life for our people. Even when China reaches the level of a moderately developed country in the middle of the twenty-first century, we will continue to try to make further strides.

This great ambition is shared by the entire Chinese people today, from the leadership down to the general public. This objective alone will keep the present generation and the next two to three generations extremely busy. To lift the life of one-fifth of the world's population to a high level is also a great responsibility. It is China's duty to shoulder that responsibility for the sake of human progress. How, then, should China achieve such an objective?

This question is a topic of debate the world over. I would argue that China's own development has answered and is answering this question, and will do so ever more convincingly in the future. The underlying fact is that in the twenty-five years since its reform and opening up, China has blazed a new strategic path that not only suits its national conditions but also conforms to the tide of the times. This new path enables China's peaceful rise by independently building socialism with Chinese characteristics while participating in, rather than isolating itself from, economic globalization.

In discussing this path, I would first like to emphasize that the decision to take part in economic globalization—instead of shunning it—in itself represents a major strategic choice. This choice was put before the Chinese people in the 1970s, when the new technological revolution and a new wave of economic globalization were gathering great momentum. The Chinese leadership grasped this trend and, deeming with great insight that today's world is an open world and China's development is inseparable from that world, decided to seize the historical opportunity and shift its focus to economic development. By endeavoring to foster domestic markets and tap international markets by implementing the household contracting system in rural areas, establishing four special economic zones in the coastal region, and opening up fourteen coastal cities, it ushered in a new period in China's reform and opening up.

In the 1990s, China was once again faced with a strategic

choice due to the Asian financial crisis and the struggle between the forces for and against globalization. The Chinese leadership carefully weighed the positives and the negatives and resolutely laid down the strategic policy of engaging in economic globalization, seeking out advantages while avoiding disadvantages. Such a move lifted China's reform and opening up to a higher level.

Second, I would point out that while participating in economic globalization, China should pursue a road of independent development. As a large developing country with a population of over 1 billion, China cannot afford and should not expect to rely on the international community. Its only option is to rely on its own strength. That is to say, it must (1) fully and consciously draw on its own institutional innovation, (2) tap the growing domestic market, (3) translate its hefty savings into investment, (4) improve the quality of its citizens' lives, and (5) address its resource shortages and environmental problems through the advancement of science and technology. In a word, to solve the major problem of development and realize our great ambition, we have to give scope to all positive factors, relying on both domestic and international markets and on resources both at home and abroad.

Third, I must emphasize that China's path is not only to strive to rise but to adhere to peace and never seek hegemony. Modern history has time and again testified to the fact that the rise of a new major power often results in dramatic change in the international configuration and the world order—it may even trigger a world war. An important reason for this outcome is that these powers have followed an aggressive path of war and expansion. Such a path is doomed to failure.

In today's world, how can Asian countries—China included—follow a path that serves nobody's interests? China's only choice is to strive to rise, and more important, to strive for a peaceful rise. That is to say, we have to work toward a peaceful international environment for the sake of our own development and at the same time safeguard world peace through this process of development.

In this respect, there are three crucial strategic principles:

—First, we must unswervingly advance economic and political reforms centering on the promotion of a socialist market economy and socialist democracy, to ensure institutional safeguards for our peaceful rise;

—Second, we must boldly draw on the fruits of all human civilization while fostering the Chinese civilization, to ensure cultural support for China's peaceful rise; and

—Third, we must carefully balance the interests of different sectors, securing a coordinated development between urban and rural areas, between different regions, between society and the economy, and between man and nature to create a social environment for China's peaceful rise.

Admittedly, over the past years China's reform and opening up have been anything but smooth sailing. We have faced many tests. The Chinese people, however, have never wavered in their resolve to embrace the new path for peaceful rise. In today's China, therefore, reform, liberalization, and peaceful development are deeply rooted in the way of life and in the culture, which in turn has created a secure environment for China's strategic path for peaceful rise.

Beginning in the 1960s and 1970s, certain Asian countries and regions have become the most dynamic areas in the world in terms of socioeconomic development. China started its own reform and opening up at the end of the 1970s, bringing about rapid economic growth and social progress. Economic ties between China and other Asian countries have become closer, and the Asian regional economy is pulling increasing weight in the global economy.

Consider economic relations and trade between China and the Association of Southeast Asian Nations (ASEAN), for example. Over the past decade, bilateral trade between the two increased by more than six times. Its value reached $54.77 billion in 2002 and is expected to top $100 billion by 2005. Meanwhile, the establishment of a China-ASEAN free trade area will herald even closer economic cooperation. As the Chinese saying goes, "A close neighbor means more than a distant relative." I am very pleased to see the new cooperative relationship of mutual promotion, mutual benefit, mutual support, and complementarity forged between China and other Asian countries.

As a scholar and an observer, I would conclude with the following judgment based on history and the current situation: generally speaking, in the coming two or three decades, or in the early twenty-first century, Asia will face a rare historical opportunity for peaceful rise, and China's peaceful rise will be a part of Asia's peaceful rise. This not only means that China's reform, opening up, and rise are partly attributable to the experience and development of other Asian countries; it also means that China, as an Asian country, will play a more active and useful role in the development, prosperity, and stability of all the other Asian countries, and its neighbors in particular.

Enough to Keep This and the Next Two to Three Generations of Chinese Extremely Busy

Interview with Anthony Yuen, Phoenix TV, November 3, 2003

TWO MATHEMATICAL PROPOSITIONS

ANTHONY YUEN: In your speech just now at the Bo'ao Forum for Asia, you used a very interesting concept, "the two mathematical propositions"—or multiplication and division—to explain China's development problems. Can you elaborate on that?

ZHENG BIJIAN: I think this is something we Chinese are living with everyday, and I have highlighted it only because it is an easy way to understand the problems China faces in its development and China's development path.

Take the "multiplication" first. Every country has its share of difficulties, troubles, and even afflictions in its development. For a relatively small country, a difficulty, trouble, or affliction is limited in scale, after all; but for a big country with 1.3 billion people, like China, things are totally different. To make an analogy, even a sesame seed multiplied by 1.3 billion will be quite a stack! Then, how about a difficulty of economic and social development multiplied by 1.3 billion? In many cases, an ordinary difficulty for another country may very well be a big problem for China's development, or even a mega-problem, a world class problem! This is what I mean by multiplication.

Now we come to the "division." China is undoubtedly a large

country with considerable material and financial resources, ranking among the top in the world in some important products. China now produces more steel than the United States and Japan put together. But once the material and financial resources are divided by 1.3 billion, the per capita level is very low indeed. A more obvious example is GDP. China is sixth in the world in terms of GDP, at about U.S. $1 trillion. But divided by 1.3 billion, the resulting per capita GDP only ranks 109th in the world! This is what I call division.

Of course, the multiplication and division both relate to difficulties and problems. If we only look at this side of the coin, there seems no way out. In fact, there is the other side, the positive side. The quarter-century of experience since the Third Plenum of the Eleventh Party Congress is forceful testament that as long as China is truly invigorated and all positive factors at home and abroad are mobilized, the big and even mega-problems that China faces in development can be resolved step by step. Hope is on our side. The large population is sometimes a heavy burden, but it also provides an abundant workforce. Once China is truly invigorated and the Chinese people's creativity fully tapped, many unimaginable things will be accomplished. Another example is purchasing power. If a large majority of our population were in a state of poverty, there would be no real purchasing power to talk about, only "potential purchasing power," at best. But the reality is the vast majority of the people are getting richer day by day and have more in their pockets to spend. This means real purchasing power! Therefore, for a populous country like ours, the workforce, creativity, and purchasing power—the factors driving economic growth—are huge and increasing. The cohesion and momentum of growth of the country will also become stronger. A big country of 1.3 billion people and with such a strong momentum for growth will undoubtedly be an engine of growth for the world, for if the Chinese market expands it will attract more goods, investment, and intellectual resources to the benefit of Asia and the world.

To sum up, we cannot talk about difficulties and problems, or driving forces on the positive side, without mentioning the factor of 1.3 billion to 1.5 billion. Where the difficulty lies, the hope of a solution also rises.

TRULY INVIGORATING CHINA

YUEN: That's a very interesting and enlightening view. And what do you believe is the key to the transformation from difficulty to driving force?

ZHENG: The key is reform. Like I said, as long as China is truly invigorated and all positive factors are mobilized, an extremely strong driving force will be fully liberated. But how can we invigorate China? The answer is reform. This has been proved by all that has happened since the Third Plenum of the Eleventh Party Congress.

The phrase "invigorate the country" was first used by Deng Xiaoping in May 1987, when he said, "It was not until December 1978, when the Central Committee of the Eleventh Party Congress convened its Third Plenary Session, that we began to invigorate the country by devoting all our energies to things the people wanted us to do."[1] He made it very clear that concentrat-

1. Deng Xiaoping, "Reform and Opening to the Outside World Can Truly Invigorate China" (May 12, 1987), in *Selected Works of Deng Xiaoping*, vol. 3 (Beijing: People's Publishing House, 1993), p. 232.

ing on economic development was the top priority, and to do that, we had to open up domestically and internationally, that is, reform. To reform is to emancipate the mind and set free the productive forces. Only when the mind is emancipated can institutions be changed and productive forces set free. And the final result will be "a China truly invigorated"!

YUEN: You talked about relying on two markets and two resources and participating in rather than remaining isolated from economic globalization. How should we understand this?

ZHENG: To China, participating in rather than isolating ourselves from economic globalization is no trivial matter; rather, it is a major strategic choice. For a very long period in the past we did not do so. There were objective causes, as well as causes of our own. The embargoes and sanctions on China were all objective causes, weren't they?

23

After the Third Plenum of the Eleventh Party Congress, the insightful Chinese leadership sensed the worldwide trend of rapid economic globalization and the related industrial restructuring, technological revolution, and capital flow. Under such circumstances, should China seize the opportunity to open to the world? The policy China adopted then was to resolutely open up to the outside world, that is, to rely on both domestic and international markets and on resources both at home and abroad and to participate in rather than remain isolated from economic globalization. That was the first strategic choice of historic significance.

In the 1990s, China was once again faced with a strategic choice, due to the Asian financial crisis and the struggle between the forces for and against globalization. Look at the crowds of demonstrators following successive meetings of the World Trade Organization all the way to Cancun and you will know what the antiglobalization movement is. While the confrontation between the forces for and against globalization posed a question to us, the Asian financial crisis confronted us in a more severe, acute, and direct manner. It is fair to say that the Asian financial crisis was a pronounced expression of the negative impact of economic globalization. During the crisis, some Southeast Asian countries suffered a lot, and in extreme cases it seemed as though the value of their assets was chopped in half! And you know how much Hong Kong lost in the crisis. In such a situation, we had to make a strategic choice—should we continue to participate in economic globalization? After sober observation and careful study of the situation, the Chinese leadership decided to continue to participate actively. At the same time, an analysis of the positive and negative aspects of economic globalization helped the leadership to lay down the policy of seeking advantages while avoiding disadvantages and the requirement of raising China's opening up to a higher level. This was the second historic strategic choice.

Therefore, in my view, an important element of China's development path is to participate in rather than remain isolated from economic globalization; the experience of the past twenty-five years has been a success. This is something we have never done before, something never seen in the history of world socialism.

YUEN: Why do you regard independent development as an important point?

ZHENG: Good question. I think the importance of this point must be emphasized. In the process of participating in rather than remaining isolated from economic globalization, we must build socialism independently with Chinese characteristics. It is of prime importance! As a country with a population of over 1.3 billion, especially as a socialist country, China cannot rely on other countries at every turn, even if it wanted to. What I mean by self-dependence is to consciously base our development on the fundamentals of our own strength; that is, the five things to rely on that I mentioned in my Bo'ao speech. Of these five things, I wish to emphasize here the tapping of domestic demand and the domestic market. It is obvious that in such a densely populated country as China, a small increase in rates of consumption will mean a big expansion in the consumer market. Given that total domestic savings currently stand at above RMB 10 trillion and are still increasing, China will enjoy a huge impetus for development if these savings can be channeled into investment alongside consumption growth.

The five things boil down to the internal vigor generated and liberated in the process of independently building socialism with Chinese characteristics plus international cooperation in the spirit of mutual benefit, on which we rely to solve the various big or even mega-problems in China's development. They also mean that China will never follow the path beaten by some other rising powers, who tried to solve their problems by seeking hegemony

through external expansion, aggressive war, and even world war.
China's domestic and foreign policies can be summarized as a
development path of peaceful rise.

THE "CHINA THREAT"

YUEN: In the process of China's rise and when its rapid economic development has attracted world attention, some foreigners, especially the so-called Blue team in the United States, have
talked about the "China threat." They say that a rising China will
sooner or later pose a threat to the United States and to the West
in general. Yet there are others who advocate the "China collapse"
theory, saying that when China rises, it will have conflicts with its
neighbors and collapse as a result. What, in your view, lies behind
these two extreme points of view?

ZHENG: It is a pleasure to discuss this question with you and
exchange views with more people from all walks of life through
Phoenix TV. I think we should first of all give a definition to the
rise of China. What we mean by this phrase is that China will
basically realize modernization in the mid-twenty-first century,
reaching the level of a moderately developed country. Such a rise
is what we usually mean by shaking off the state of underdevelopment and realizing the great rejuvenation of the Chinese
nation. How many years does this take? It takes 100 years if we
start counting from the founding of the People's Republic of
China, or seventy years from the Third Plenum of the Eleventh
Party Congress. We have now spent twenty-five of those seventy,
so it will take another forty-five years.

To sum up, to bring about a better life for the 1.3 to 1.5 billion
people in China is a great ambition, which alone will keep this

generation and the next two to three generations of Chinese people extremely busy.

YUEN: Your remarks make us realize that people in China are working hard on all fronts to improve their national strength. I think the future is very bright if we follow this path. Now let's look at some other countries, some developed countries in particular, that believe the rise of China will pose a threat to them. How should we dispel such misgivings?

ZHENG: The basic points to consider here are, first, the actual deeds; and second, the strategic path. What counts is your act, not your word. If you seek expansion and hegemony, whatever you say to the contrary will be lies! Besides, there is the question of strategic path. Through the twenty-five years of experience since the Third Plenum of the Eleventh Party Congress, we Chinese have blazed a path of peaceful rise, which is to build socialism with Chinese characteristics independently, while participating in rather than isolating ourselves from economic globalization. This is a strategic deployment and strategic path based on successful experience and careful consideration, it is not merely an expression of good intentions, and certainly not just diplomatic language. We hope to continue to win the understanding of more and more foreign friends with the facts and the various aspects of this strategic path.

27

Now I will talk about the question of "threat" or "peace"? This is a heavy topic for the Chinese. For more than a century, starting from 1840, China was threatened, bullied, invaded, and exploited, with tens of millions of casualties. Her history has been heavy, indeed! I think China is the only big country ever to have been subjected to so much devastation from wars of invasion in modern times. Given such a history of suffering, the Chinese want nothing but the important basics; that is, independence, unification, peace, and development. At the same time, the Chinese have observed in a sober-minded manner the serious consequences of big-power rivalries in modern history. One can see that the rise of new powers in this period often resulted in drastic changes in the international configuration and world order, leading to turbulence or even world war. Why? Because they took the old-style path of industrialization and had to compete for resources through external expansion, aggressive war, and the pursuit of hegemony. Such a path leads nowhere but to failure; it serves nobody's interests. How can China follow such an erroneous path in the twenty-first century? It has never taken that path, nor will it ever do so in the future!

In a word, China has made a fundamental, historic, and strategic choice to take the development path of peaceful rise; that is, to seek a peaceful environment for our development, and to safeguard peace with our development, in turn. We have benefited a lot from following this path, and there is no reason why we shouldn't continue down it.

CHINA'S PEACEFUL RISE
AND OPPORTUNITIES FOR
THE ASIA-PACIFIC REGION

Bo'ao Forum for Asia and
China Reform Forum Roundtable Meeting,
April 18, 2004

The China Reform Forum and the Bo'ao Forum for Asia have come together to discuss the important relationship between China's peaceful rise and economic globalization. Due to China's development, over the past two years "China threat" and "China collapse" have become hot topics in some countries. I have noticed lately that people are also quite interested in the topic of China's peaceful rise and have raised some very thought-provoking questions that deserve answers. I would like to elaborate on three aspects of this issue: the nature and feasibility of China's path to peaceful rise; what China's peaceful rise will bring to the Asia-Pacific region; and where the future of China and the Asia-Pacific region lies.

Before I discuss the path of China's peaceful rise, some clarification is in order. This term refers to the development strategy dating back to the Third Plenum of the Eleventh Congress of the Chinese Communist Party (CCP), at the end of 1978, and lasting until the middle of the twenty-first century. In this long-term process, with peace and development remaining the themes of the times, China by and large has been realizing modernization through sustained, rapid, coordinated, and sound development on the basis of reform and opening up. It has been a quarter of a century since China embarked on the road to peaceful rise. Deng Xiaoping, the chief architect of China's reform and opening up, set us on this road, and it is under the leadership of Jiang Zemin, the core of China's third-generation leadership, and Hu Jintao, the leader of the new generation, that we stride forward into the twenty-first century.

The past twenty-five years have been quite extraordinary. Our biggest achievement is to have realized that peace and rise, which look quite contradictory, can actually be integrated. In the past, the rise of a big power often involved toppling the international order and threatening peace. China breaks this rule. While seeking a peaceful international environment to ensure our development, we are safeguarding world peace through our own development. How do we manage to integrate peace and rise? If there is any secret formula, it is that we have blazed a trail by building our own socialism with Chinese characteristics, while engaging in, rather than isolating ourselves from, economic globalization.

By engaging in economic globalization, I mean we have not only opened our domestic markets, but also tapped world markets under the rubric of peaceful coexistence with the rest of the world. We seek a win-win, mutually beneficial situation by competing on a level playing field with other countries, under the same rules and on the principle of making the most of given advantages while avoiding disadvantages. Building socialism independently with Chinese characteristics reflects the fact that, while we attach importance to utilizing world markets and the resources they provide, we mainly depend on our own strengths to resolve the problems that arise in the process of development, rather than allowing these troubles to spread to other countries. As a big country, covering a large area and endowed with rich natural resources, China is capable of achieving such a goal.

Two Chinese sayings may help illustrate this process:

—"Do not do to others what you would not have them do to you," and

—"He who helps others helps himself."

This is how peaceful rise comes about.

The main worry of those who doubt the feasibility of the path for peaceful rise chosen by the Chinese people is that in the first decades of the twenty-first century, China is faced with both opportunities and challenges. How can China handle them all? It is true that we do not face smooth sailing; there will be both predictable and unpredictable challenges, risks, and pressures. Indeed, not only are we soberly aware of this situation, but we have formed a scientific approach to dealing with these opportunities and challenges:

—First, experience tells us that there is no free lunch. To seize and create opportunities and open up new perspectives, we have to overcome difficulties and cope with risks.

—Second, our experience has also shown that while opportunities and challenges may be brought about by both domestic and foreign factors, the decisive factor is always China itself. Our success depends on whether we are able to seize the opportunities with a pioneering spirit and refrain from blindly following the beaten track.

—Third, given China's weakness compared to many big powers in the world, coupled with a host of serious problems, we are certainly faced with quite a lot of unpredictable factors and difficulties. So long as we handle these weaknesses properly, and find new approaches and strategies, we will be able to turn risks into opportunities, and even create new opportunities.

All in all, these internal and external factors, these positive and negative aspects, and our attitude toward opportunities dictate that in the first two decades of the twenty-first century, while confronting various risks and challenges, China will usher in a new era of strategic opportunity for its peaceful rise.

What will China's peaceful rise bring to the Asia-Pacific region? Last year at this forum I mentioned two questions of mathematics, one concerning multiplication, the other, division. They illustrate the pressures and impetus that China's huge population bring to development and prove that we have to concentrate on our own development.

Here, I put forward two more mathematical propositions. One concerns addition, the other concerns subtraction:

—Adding a big market of 1.3 billion people and China's rapidly growing economy to the Asia-Pacific economy will produce huge growth potential; and

—Subtracting the Chinese market of 1.3 billion people from the Asia-Pacific market will produce a huge market vacuum.

That is to say, China's peaceful rise and the sustained, rapid, coordinated, and sound growth of its economy will bring about tremendous historic opportunities, not threats, to the Asia-Pacific region.

These opportunities are the product of China's independent foreign policy and its pursuit of a path of peaceful rise. China is already a constructive force for peace and stability in the region, rather than a destructive force that challenges the regional order. Having suffered from a scourge of wars and civil conflicts, the Chinese people know full well that peace is precious and that development is important. China will participate in all that is conducive to the stability and peace of the Asia-Pacific region and will strongly oppose all that is detrimental to regional stability and destructive of regional peace. This is fully borne out by China's responsible behavior in handling regional affairs.

These historic opportunities are also the result of the various subregional cooperation mechanisms and close economic links that China has forged with its neighbors in the process of its peaceful rise. This system not only serves the needs of the developing countries involved, but also provides a platform for big powers to play their due roles in the region. The subregional system and U.S. alignments with its Asian allies, though distinct, are not confrontational; rather, they can be complementary and reinforcing in promoting stability in the region.

China's culture and traditions, and its historical influence in the Asia-Pacific region, also give rise to tremendous opportunities. An ancient civilization with a history of several thousand years, China has a tradition of inclusiveness and drawing on others' strong points. In particular, it has very deep-seated historical and cultural links with other East Asian countries. China's cultural tradition, featuring "unity in diversity" and "priority to peace," also goes a long way toward facilitating China's harmonious coexistence and sharing of prosperity with the Asia-Pacific region and the world at large.

In general, China's peaceful rise brings to the Asia-Pacific region opportunities for development, conditions for peace, and space for cooperation. Moreover, we believe that China and the Asia-Pacific countries have much to offer each other. The more opportunities we give to the Asia-Pacific countries, the more opportunities we get from them. If China fails to provide oppor-

tunities for Asia-Pacific countries as it develops, China will lose
its opportunity for peaceful rise. With this basic understanding,
China will never become a threat to the region. There is no deny-
ing that China's peaceful rise will somewhat intensify competition in the region. But this competition is characterized by
friendship, cooperation, mutual benefit, and a win-win ideal; it is
not the competition of an arms buildup or for spheres of influence or hegemony. None of us should miscalculate strategically
on this point.

I now turn to the future of China and the Asia-Pacific region.
At present, the world is undergoing tremendous and profound
changes. With peace and development remaining the themes of
the times, the Asia-Pacific region has more development opportunities than do other regions in the world as big-power relationships are realigned. China's peaceful rise, in particular, will
contribute to the creation of a win-win situation and common
prosperity. This will be the general trend of the region in the first
couple of decades of the twenty-first century.

I would note, first, that the Asia-Pacific countries are blessed
with opportunities brought about by the strong economic
growth of the region as a whole. Compared with most other
regions, the Asia-Pacific region has fewer wars and conflicts, and
most countries are committed to their own development. To
share these opportunities, the Asia-Pacific region, and East Asia
in particular, needs to form communities of common interests.

Second, the new threats that we face come mainly from nontraditional security areas. Such comprehensive and profound
challenges cannot be met with the strength of a single country. It
will take our joint efforts to guard against and dissolve current
and prospective threats; that is to say, cooperation is the effective

way to maintain security in the Asia-Pacific region. As mentioned above, common challenges facing China and the Asia-Pacific countries create the need to establish multilayered communities of specific common interests that are conducive to all parties. In particular, maintaining cooperative partnerships among big countries, establishing an early warning and crisis management mechanism for big countries, and expanding their common interests to guarantee common security have become prerequisites for regional, and even world, peace.

Third, it is necessary to emphasize that in the process of its peaceful rise, China has formed a new security concept that differs from any traditional concept. With mutual trust, mutual benefit, equality, and cooperation as its core notions, our new paradigm firmly abandons the strategic framework in which big powers in the past vied for spheres of influence, engaged in military confrontation, or exported ideologies. Ours is a comprehensive and strategic concept with peaceful coexistence as its precondition, common interest as its basis, strategic cooperation as its bond, and common development as its objective. History and experience have repeatedly proved that armed forces cannot make peace and that power politics cannot ensure security. The collective security achieved through cooperation among the Asia-Pacific countries will surely lead to universal, lasting peace and rapid, sustained development.

Finally, we are soberly aware that given the huge area, large population, and great differences in systems and cultures, it will take arduous efforts and a long time to realize full regional integration and build comprehensive regional mechanisms. Nonetheless, as a starting point, the establishment of a variety of subregional mechanisms and flexible cooperation could achieve marked results. For instance, the northeast Asian subregion might set collective security as its goal and the southeast subregion might mainly target market integration and trade liberalization, while the northwest subregion might focus on counterterrorism and economic cooperation.

All in all, the future of China and the Asia-Pacific region hinges on lasting peace, sustained development, and cooperation. We are confident that so long as we work hand in hand, pull together, and do not falter, the Asia-Pacific region, and East Asia in particular, will surely have a promising future.

CHINA'S DEVELOPMENT AND
NEW PATH TO A PEACEFUL RISE

Villa d'Este Forum, September 2004

China's rapid development in recent years has attracted wide attention, and its rise has become a hot topic in the international community. The key issue is how to perceive China's future development in the first half of the twenty-first century. Here, I would like to share my observations on the following topics: how to perceive China's achievements in development; and how to perceive China's path of development in the first half of the twenty-first century.

To illustrate China's development achievements over the past twenty-five years, I offer some statistics. China adopted its policy of reform and opening up in 1978. Since that time, it has been one of the most rapidly growing economies in the world, as evidenced by an average annual gross domestic product (GDP) growth rate of 9.4 percent. In 1978 China accounted for less than 1 percent of the world economy; that share has now grown to 4 percent. In 1978 China's total external trade volume stood at $20.6 billion; last year it was forty times larger, at $851.2 billion, and ranked third in the world. A dozen years ago China had barely entered the age of modern telecommunications services. Now, it has 296 million mobile phone subscribers, more than any other country in the world. And as of June this year, 87 million people had access to the Internet and 36.3 million computers were connected to the web. These figures demonstrate that China has made solid progress in economic and overall national strength in the past quarter of a century. However, economic growth alone cannot tell the full story.

At the annual session of the Bo'ao Forum for Asia held in Hainan, China, last year, I cited two simple mathematic propositions that illustrate the implications of China's basic national condition—a big population of 1.3 billion. Any small difficulty in economic and social development multiplied by 1.3 billion swells into a huge problem. And any amount of financial and material resources, however large, divided by 1.3 billion, shrinks to a tiny handful in per capita terms.

Without a doubt, in aggregate terms China is an economic power whose rapid growth is felt by the whole world. Yet China's economy in 2003 was just one-seventh the size of the U.S. economy and one-third the size of Japan's. In per capita terms, China is still a low-income developing country, ranking below one-hundredth in the world. Our impact on the world economy is limited, after all. Therefore, in the final analysis, all of our efforts to resolve problems of development focus on bettering the lives of our 1.3 billion—or even 1.5 billion—people, and creating an increasingly more prosperous and civilized environment, suitable for their comprehensive development. This work alone will keep several generations of the Chinese people quite busy.

At present, the international community is very concerned about China's "overheating economy." It is my view that while the economy on the whole is sound, its structure has yet to be rationalized. Serious problems in agriculture, energy, the environment, and investment are cropping up in the course of development. Therefore, since the middle of last year, the Chinese government has adopted a series of macroeconomic control measures to address questions of structure, system, and the growth model. Macroeconomic control has yielded initial results, and grain production has taken a sharp turn for the better. Furthermore, the macroeconomic policy environment is becoming increasingly relaxed. And it is important to note that despite macroeconomic control, China's economy will still grow by 8 to 9 percent this year—yet another indication of its great potential.

On the question of how to perceive China's path of development in the first half of the twenty-first century, I have several points to make. First, China's path to a peaceful rise refers to its path toward socialist modernization. This journey will span seventy years, from the end of the 1970s, when the Third Plenum of the Eleventh Congress of the Chinese Communist Party adopted the policy of reform and opening up, to the middle of the twenty-first century, when basic modernization will be realized. That is to say, we have been marching on this path for twenty-five years, and another forty-five years are ahead of us before China rises as a basically modernized and medium-level developed country.

We term this path toward modernization "a development path to a peaceful rise" because in contrast to some other emerging powers in modern history, who plundered other countries of their resources through invasion, expansion, or even large-scale wars of aggression, China will acquire the capital, technology, and resources needed for its modernization by peaceful means. The continuous rapid development that China has witnessed in the past twenty-five years proves that we have been quite successful in pursuing this path. This undoubtedly deserves attention.

For China to acquire resources through peaceful means, it is extremely important that it open up to the rest of the world; namely, to integrate itself into, instead of isolating itself from, economic globalization. As we open up, we also carry out all-around reforms and engage in a market economy at home. As a result, more than $500 billion have flowed in from overseas, domestic nongovernmental investment amounted to over RMB 10 trillion, and the huge pool of state-owned assets has been revitalized. This is what we call use of "two markets and two resources," both domestic and overseas.

Yet even as we open wider to the outside world and integrate into economic globalization, we uphold the principle of independence in building socialism with Chinese characteristics. On the one hand, we need to gain access to much-needed capital, technology, and resources in world markets by engaging in mutually beneficial competition on an equal footing. On the other hand, we must not depend too much on world markets, and even less, cause panic. We believe in acting on the basis of our own strengths. In other words, we address the issue of development through new ideas and institutional innovations, by industrial restructuring, exploring the growing domestic market, transferring huge personal savings into investment, and developing our human resources in greater depth and magnitude—that is, upgrading people's capacities and expediting scientific progress.

As China enters the twenty-first century, it faces three big development challenges. The first is that of natural resources. Currently, China's exploitable oil and natural gas reserves, water resources, and arable land are all well below world averages in per capita terms. The second challenge is the environment. Serious pollution, the wasteful use of resources, and low rates of recycling are bottlenecks for sustainable economic development. The third is the lack of coordination between economic and social development. These three major challenges, alongside rapid growth, mean that China is facing both a golden period of development and a period of tough choices. China is once again at a critical juncture. To attain our goal of building a well-off society that benefits all, we need to do the following:

—Deepen and continue to press ahead with comprehensive reform in economic, political, and cultural institutions;

—Formulate comprehensive plans to coordinate development in rural and urban areas, development in different regions, economic and social development, environmental improvement, and domestic development and opening up; and

—Pursue sustainable development.

In short, we need to concentrate on domestic efforts, rely on scientific and technological revolution and a new path of industrialization, and lay equal emphasis on opening up more sources of income and cutting down expenses, while at the same time promoting international cooperation on energy, resource management, and environmental protection to achieve mutually beneficial results.

Another huge risk and challenge is, of course, the issue of Taiwan. The path to a peaceful rise, by definition, requires the peaceful reunification of Taiwan and mainland China and is conducive to it. As long as there is still the slightest hope, no effort shall be spared to achieve this goal. However, should proponents of Taiwan's independence defy the wishes of the international community, or should foreign forces dare to intervene to support Taiwan's independence, the use of force will by no means be ruled out. However, even if the use of force becomes inevitable, it should certainly not be understood as an act of invasion, but as, by any measure, a righteous move to safeguard national unity and territorial integrity against separatist activities.

In striving for a peaceful international environment, particularly with regard to the international order and its regimes, China turns its back on the old practices of modern emerging powers breaking down existing international systems through war and seeking hegemony through bloc confrontation. China does not seek hegemony and predominance, nor will it toe the line of others. It advocates a new road toward a new international political and economic order by reforming and democratizing international relations. It maintains world peace for its own development, which in turn reinforces world peace. China is a constructive—not destructive—force for peace and stability.

I reiterate that in speaking of a peaceful rise, I am referring to peaceful development, which is one of the defining characteristics of Chinese socialism. China has made history in two respects: First, as an emerging major country, China has transcended the old path of industrialization characterized by rivalry for resources and bloody wars, and has chosen to rise peacefully through sustainable development. This is unprecedented. Second, China has transcended the cold war mentality that rejects peaceful development and cooperation on the grounds of differences in social systems and ideologies. China is rising peacefully and independently, building a socialism with Chinese characteristics through brave reforms and opening up—in other words, by integrating into the world economy rather than isolating itself. This, again, is unprecedented.

Thus, for all the reasons given above, China's path to a peaceful rise and peaceful development brings to the international community opportunities, not threats. Last year, China's imports from the Association of Southeast Asian Nations and the Republic of Korea increased by more than 50 percent; from Japan and the European Union, by nearly 40 percent; and from the United States, by 24.3 percent. A peacefully rising China provides a broad market for the international community. By 2020, when China's per capita GDP will reach $3,000, its market will offer even greater potential.

Lastly, China is not the only country that is rising peacefully. As we enter the twenty-first century, we are happy to see that a number of countries are following suit by different means, with different models, and at different paces. At the same time, the developed countries are further developing themselves. There is a new trend of peace and development in the world today. I believe we should all welcome this trend.

WE SHOULD WELCOME IT

Interview with Ye Xiaoshen, writer, September 10, 2004

YE XIAOSHEN: The theory of China's peaceful rise was proposed by you at the last annual conference of the Bo'ao Forum for Asia. Were there any special reasons for choosing that occasion?

ZHENG BIJIAN: Bo'ao is a very good occasion. The Bo'ao Forum for Asia is the first international conference organization headquartered in China. We all feel it is significant to join the discussion on "Asia Searching for Win-Win, Development through Cooperation" by introducing the proposition of "China's development path of peaceful rise" at such an unofficial, not-for-profit, open, and institutionalized forum. By introducing this development path, which we have followed for twenty-five years and will continue to pursue in the twenty-first century, to all people of vision who care about the future of China and to more than 1,200 delegates from more than thirty countries and world regions, we have refuted the "China threat" theory with the peaceful nature of China's rise and responded to questions about China's "collapse" with our confidence that China will surely rise, given a peaceful environment.

MULTIPLICATION AND DIVISION

YE: I remember that in the 1970s, one of the top three American columnists, Joseph Alsop, once predicted that no matter how splendid its economic achievement might be, China would risk having its entire accomplishment written off if it failed to control the birth rate. Now, you have emphasized the population pressure while expounding on China's economic might and overall national strength, and you mentioned a question of multiplication and one of division. Why put it that way? Why take these two simple mathematic propositions as the basic point of China's peaceful rise?

ZHENG: Everyone knows that China has become the world's fastest growing economy, with an average annual GDP growth rate of 9.4 percent, since its reform and opening up. China accounted for less than 1 percent of the world's GDP in 1978 and now that share has grown to 4 percent. China had a total foreign trade volume of U.S. $20.6 billion back in 1978; that had grown to U.S. $851.2 billion last year, third in the world. Therefore, concrete progress has been made in China's economy and overall national strength in the past quarter of a century. However, economic growth alone does not represent the whole picture. I hope our friends can also see the other side of the story, the basic national condition of China, which Deng Xiaoping often expressed as, "China is so big a country, with so large a population." The true picture is that China is an economic giant in terms of GDP and has an impact on the world because of its rapid economic development. Yet even in these terms, China was only one-seventh the size of the United States and one-third the size of Japan in 2003. In terms of per capita GDP, China ranks lower than 100th in the world and is still a low-income developing country with limited influence on the world economy. All in all, I wish to explain that China still faces major difficulties and a series of very large problems in its development. So, instead of talking about how great China is or China's rise, I started by talking about our problems and difficulties in development, about how hard it is for China to rise.

Of course, following those remarks, I highlighted our confidence in spite of the magnitude of the difficulties and immense challenges. We are confident because we have blazed a new path with our own successful practice. It is—in a term that can be understood by all people at home and abroad, whatever their ideological background—a "development path of peaceful rise." It is the path of socialism with Chinese characteristics, the path of realizing socialist modernization in China, and the path of the great rejuvenation of the Chinese nation. Just to continue along this path, to shake off the state of underdevelopment completely, and to offer all our people a better material and cultural life, could keep the current and the next two to three generations of Chinese people, from top leaders to ordinary citizens, extremely busy.

YE: Why did you say "two to three generations"? Deng Xiaoping was talking about "several, a dozen, or maybe dozens of generations," wasn't he?

ZHENG: It's great that you noticed this point. Deng Xiaoping talked about "the unrelenting endeavor of several, a dozen, or maybe dozens of generations" when he traveled to southern China in 1992. It is, definitely, a significant point. But please note that Deng was referring to the entire socialist period; in his words, "It takes a long historical period to consolidate and develop socialism." That's the context in which he drew the important conclusion that "it requires the unrelenting endeavor of several, a dozen, or maybe dozens of generations." What we are talking about here is building China into a moderately developed country within a century from the founding of the People's Republic, or basically realizing modernization by the mid-twenty-first century, starting from the Third Plenum of the Eleventh Party Congress. The two should not be confused. How many years are there between the Third Plenum and the middle of the twenty-first century, then? Seventy. We have traversed twenty-five years and there are still forty-five ahead. Then, let's do some mathematics. Sixty years will be two generations' time (if we count a generation as thirty years), which is to say, it will take two generations from now to basically realize modernization in China. It would still be shy of three generations if we started counting from the Third Plenum, for that would be seventy years. This is why I have emphasized more than once that it would keep this and the next two to three generations of Chinese people extremely busy to provide a good life for our population of 1.3 to 1.5 billion.

47

CHINESE CHARACTERISTICS MEANS
TWO TRANSCENDINGS

YE: You mentioned a time frame of seventy years in relation to keeping two to three generations extremely busy. What's the rationale for such a time frame? Why couldn't we push back the starting point of the path to realize socialist modernization in China? Zhou Enlai mentioned the "four modernizations" in his government work report at the Third National People's Congress in 1964, to which Mao Zedong added, "We must break away from the beaten tracks and adopt advanced technologies to the best of our capacity, so as to build China into a modernized socialist power within not too long a period of time." Zhou reiterated the four modernizations in his 1975 government work report at the Fourth National People's Congress, didn't he?

ZHENG: You've again made a good observation. As I said just now, it would take us about a century to realize China's socialist modernization if you start counting from the founding of the People's Republic in 1949. However, the path of socialist modernization for China that we are talking about here is not a broad concept; instead, it refers exclusively to the new path opened up by the Third Plenum of the Eleventh Party Congress. It is a new path because of the reform and opening up, a "Chinese characteristic" that was only fully unfolded after the Third Plenum.

It is now becoming more and more clear that Chinese characteristics means "two transcendings." First, it means to transcend the old road to industrialization, which entails a worldwide struggle for resources. Our approach is to realize a peaceful rise through a new path toward industrialization, through sustainable development, which is unprecedented in modern world history. Second, it means to transcend the cold war mentality centered on hegemony, which rejects peace, development, and cooperation on the grounds of differences in social system and ideology. We have practiced reform and opening up courageously in building socialism with Chinese characteristics and marching toward a peaceful rise independently—by participating in rather than isolating ourselves from economic globalization and by learning, borrowing and absorbing all achievements of human civilization. This path, again, is unprecedented in modern world history. The path we are blazing is brand new, since our two transcendings have no precedent. We have been on this path for a quarter of a century and we still have forty-five years until the mid-twenty-first century, when we will realize basic socialist modernization, or in other words, the great rejuvenation of the Chinese nation and the peaceful rise of China.

Is seven decades too long a period for China, a country with 1.3 to 1.5 billion people, which used to be rather underdeveloped both economically and culturally, to achieve this objective? I think not. Seventy years, or even a century, if we count from the founding of the People's Republic, is not too long for such a task. In the world's economic history, it took two and a half centuries from the onset of the industrial revolution to industrialize 1.5 billion people! That's why I once said, if China achieves industrialization and informatization in one hundred years, it will be by far the largest, most profound, and most rapid social transformation the world has ever seen.

TO TRANSCEND THE OLD ROAD TO INDUSTRIALIZATION

YE: If I remember correctly, the "new road to industrialization" was first proposed at the Sixteenth Party Congress, when "modernization" and the "new road to industrialization" were organically linked. It was stated that "it remains an arduous historical task in the process of our drive to modernization to accomplish industrialization. IT application is a logical choice if the industrialization and modernization of our country are to be accelerated. It is, therefore, necessary to persist in using IT to propel industrialization, which will, in turn, stimulate IT application, blazing a new trail to industrialization featuring high scientific and technological content, good economic returns, low resource consumption, little environmental pollution, and a full display of advantages in human resources." I wonder if you are referring to the new road to industrialization when you talk of transcending the old road to industrialization?

ZHENG: That's right. The new road to industrialization was clearly put forward at the Sixteenth Party Congress, when development was given top priority in "governing and rejuvenating the country." But how could this be done? Sustainable development through the new road to industrialization is the answer. It is a question of vital importance pertaining to the future direction of China. China is a developing country, but its sheer size makes its road to industrialization a matter not only for China itself, but also for the whole world. In fact, in recent years some new issues arising in our foreign trade, demand for resources, foreign investment, and environmental pollution have drawn widespread attention.

YE: I think the aggravating world energy crisis has sounded the alarm for China's international strategy time and again. As the reform goes deeper, China opens wider to the world, and globalization picks up speed, not only do China's products rely more and more on the world market, but China's domestic development also increasingly depends on resources from outside. However, our international strategy seems still to lag behind the need, for the external resources crucial to our national development are more often than not controlled by others, and their supply would be in dire danger in the event of any contingency.

ZHENG: The key point here is how to solve these problems while continuing on our road to industrialization and modernization. We cannot take the beaten track to industrialization that was trodden by quite a few late risers in modern world history, resulting in nothing but detriment to all and grave disaster for humanity as a whole. What is that old path to industrialization? Put in simple terms, it is unconstrained consumption of resources; and when domestic supply falls short of demand, it would rob other parts of the world, through colonization, aggression, expansion, and even world war. The two world wars in the first half of the twentieth century were both triggered by this fundamental cause. We definitely will not take this road. As a rising country in the twenty-first century, China has to transcend this road by pursuing a new path to industrialization. We need to properly solve the problems of resources and environment through sustainable development, relying primarily on our domestic resources, finding new supplies while using resources economically. At the same time, we will rely on international cooperation on resource and environment issues based on "win-win" (bilateral) and "all-win" (multilateral) principles, so as to obtain the funding, technology, and resources needed for modernization by peaceful means. This is unprecedented in modern world history. Is it not a peaceful rise? In fact, the sustained and rapid progress of China during the past twenty-five years of reform and opening up, while participating in rather than isolating ourselves from economic globalization, has already given initial proof that such a road to development is viable. We have become more conscious and clear about this with the Sixteenth Party Congress and in the twenty-first century.

YE: Could you elaborate on how it is possible for us to obtain the external resources needed for our modernization through peaceful means?

ZHENG: On the one hand, we have to obtain external resources through peaceful means because of the historical traditions and socialist nature of China. On the other hand, one extremely important condition for us to be able to do so is our opening up to the outside world, our participation in rather than isolation from economic globalization. It should be noted that we started our full-blown reform and opening up in the late 1970s, when peace and development became the main theme of the times and the third wave of globalization in the history of humanity was in full swing. Only under such unique historical conditions could we get the necessary external resources from the world market on the basis of self-reliance. In this sense, it could also be said that globalization has made China's peaceful rise possible. With our reform and opening up, we have attracted more than U.S. $500 billion of overseas investment, formed over RMB 10 trillion of capital, and reinvigorated immense state assets. This is the utilization of both domestic and international markets and resources.

TO TRANSCEND THE COLD WAR MENTALITY

YE: My intuitive notion of the cold war mentality is the use of traditional, especially cold war, thinking to handle new security threats, which is obviously wrong. However, some worry that if we wish to transcend this mentality while it is still widespread in the world, we will put ourselves at a disadvantage. What's your view?

ZHENG: The cold war mentality is the stubborn pursuit and practice of hegemony and the rejection of peace, development, and cooperation on the grounds of differences in social system and ideology. We are clear that even when peace and development have become the themes of our times, the cold war mentality and various other threats to security will continue to exist. That's why we have always been highly vigilant, sticking to an independent stance and always striving to boost our economic might, overall national strength, and national defense capability. Do we have to follow suit if there is still a cold war mentality in the world today? Of course not! I think it should be just the opposite. The more of the cold war mentality there is in the world, the higher we need to hold up the banner of peace, development, and cooperation. Deng Xiaoping pointed out clearly in October 1989 that each country should "proceed from its own long-term strategic interests, and at the same time respect the interests of the other. Each country, whether it is big or small, strong or weak, should respect others as equals, giving no thought to old scores or to differences in social systems and ideologies."[1] Following this direction, we should hold high the banner of peace, development, and cooperation, relying on ourselves to build socialism with Chinese characteristics, participating in rather than isolating ourselves from economic globalization, and thus realizing socialist modernization and the great rejuvenation of the Chinese nation—in other words, China's peaceful rise. In this sense, China's peaceful rise and peaceful development are one and the same thing.

53

As for our task of building up national defense while holding high the banner of peace, development, and cooperation, it is absolutely coherent! It is only right and proper that we do not rule out the use of force in case the "Taiwan independence" forces split our country or some foreign forces interfere and support

1. Deng Xiaoping, "The United States Should Take the Initiative in Putting an End to the Strains in Sino-American Relations" (October 31, 1989), in *Selected Works of Deng Xiaoping,* vol. 3, 1st ed. (Beijing: People's Publishing House, 1993), p. 330.

Taiwan independence. And it is only logical that we undertake justifiable defense when we are invaded! It is fair to say that these are all reasonable implications of China's development path of peaceful rise!

For the same reason, when we identify peace and security as the theme of the times we do not ignore the fact that the world is far from tranquil and various security threats do exist. But should the existence of regional conflicts and contingencies in the world change the fundamental scientific evaluation of the theme of the times? Definitely not! The mainstream prevails!

PEACEFUL RISE IS THE SAME AS
PEACEFUL DEVELOPMENT

YE: Why do you say that peaceful rise and peaceful development are actually the same? Isn't *rise* more expressive than *development*?

ZHENG: Different words are needed for different contexts and occasions. It's fine to choose either of the two terms, as long as it fits the context.

YE: Are you saying we should focus more on the essence?

ZHENG: Good question. The problem is that sometimes we don't have a deep understanding or awareness. In my view, according to Deng Xiaoping's profound thinking, the strategic planning and the path that China has blazed since the Third Plenum of the Eleventh Party Congress should be two-pronged—internal and external—and not merely about foreign policy. In Deng Xiaoping's words, there are two kinds of overall situation, domestic and international, which should be observed and analyzed together. How is the overall domestic situation of China defined? In the final analysis, it is the primary stage of socialism, the reform and opening up, and the concentration on development. How is the overall international situation defined? In the final analysis, peace and development are the biggest strategic issues or the main themes of today's world. Taken together, the two aspects lead to Deng Xiaoping's deeper understanding of socialism and the formation of a series of theories and strategies. Deng Xiaoping summarized it thus: "The socialism we are building is a socialism that helps to constantly develop the productive forces and that favors peace."[2] He said this in 1989. I think this is a very important conclusion because it expresses in the most condensed language the result of his observation and analysis of both the domestic and the international situations and raises clearly the question of what kind of socialism China is building. First, "a socialism that helps to constantly develop the productive forces" speaks of no ordinary development, but a continued and certainly rapid development. Second, "a socialism that favors peace" indicates that the rapid development of China must be closely linked with the quest for peace. These are the two basic aspects of socialism with Chinese characteristics. I therefore think that the term "a development path of peaceful rise" is in essence an extension and summary of the two basic aspects of socialism with Chinese characteristics. It is also a more expressive and useful term, one that an international audience from different ideological backgrounds can more easily understand and accept.

2. Deng Xiaoping, "No One Can Shake Socialist China" (October 26, 1989), in *Selected Works of Deng Xiaoping,* vol. 3, p. 328.

YE: Why do you say that the term "a development path of peaceful rise" is more expressive and useful to an international audience?

ZHENG: At the end of 2002, just months after the Sixteenth Party Congress, I led a delegation of the China Reform Forum to the United States. When I talked with people both inside and outside the government, I realized that two theories, namely "China threat" and "China collapse," were rather popular there. The China threat is that if China moves ahead and becomes stronger, it will vie for resources and seek expansion; while proponents of China's collapse believe that China cannot sustain its development and will finally collapse. My immediate reaction was that a reply was needed, and that I could and should respond based on the facts and basic experience of China's development. So, I began with the Sixteenth Party Congress. I told them that the congress summed up the experience that China had gained over the past twenty-odd years since the Third Plenum of the Eleventh Party Congress. What was this experience? It was reform and opening up, the essence of which is to participate in rather than being isolated from economic globalization. The path we have blazed in this way is to build socialism with Chinese characteristics independently. In this process, we cannot follow the example of some rising powers that triggered worldwide conflict in their competition for resources. Nor can we seek hegemony and reject peace, development, and cooperation because of differences in social systems and ideologies. I also pointed out that China had been on this road for twenty-five years, which testified to our commitment to peace (rather than posing any "threat") and our rapid development (rather than heading toward "collapse"). This would continue in the future, and we would only do better. These remarks were understood and well received by many Americans. So when I returned to China, I suggested that this topic be the subject of research. We have already achieved some results and I think the findings will be constantly enriched as China's development goes on.

In brief, China will realize its basic modernization, become a moderately developed country and bring about a good life for its 1.3 to 1.5 billion people, in seventy years. This is no ordinary development nor an ordinary rejuvenation. This is what we call a "great rejuvenation." Doesn't a great rejuvenation coupled with rapid development qualify as a "rise"? History will prove that our concept of a development path of peaceful rise conforms with reality. As long as we stick to it, we will have more and more friends and sympathizers, and we will have better prospects.

TO WIN A SAY ON CHINA'S DEVELOPMENT PATH

Ye: You have talked about China's development path in the United States, addressed the Bo'ao Forum twice, and given a speech titled "China's Development and New Path to a Peaceful Rise" at the thirtieth Villa d'Este Forum in Italy on September 3, 2004. All of these presentations were well received internationally. Could you give us more details?

Zheng: I think the term "a development path of peaceful rise" is well received mainly because it is easy to understand. It avoids ideological obstacles and proceeds from a realistic assessment of China's problems in development. Normally, it is hard for people of different ideological backgrounds to understand each other.

But the concept of peaceful rise is very simple, readily understandable, and makes good sense. Many foreigners, including political dignitaries and Nobel laureates, have responded positively, impressed by the sense of self-reflection and self-awareness; especially that China, a big and fast-growing country, is being sensitive to the situation of others as well as its own. From my experience over more than a year, I can see that it works. It helps us gain more understanding, sympathy, and support; helps us have a say on China's road to development; helps us get our voice heard in the world; and helps us refute with facts the theories of China threat and China collapse.

YE: It is reported that you met former U.S. president George Bush at the Bo'ao Forum. He said China was devoted to the cause of peaceful rise, which was important to Asia's landscape. Are these his own words or a summary?

ZHENG: I did talk with George Bush during the second Bo'ao Forum for Asia. Afterward, in his speech at the luncheon, he said that "the current [Chinese] leadership is committed to what we call a peaceful rise, and that's very reassuring and very, very important to the Asian horizon and Asia's landscape."

DUAL CHALLENGES, DUAL OPPORTUNITIES

YE: Although the use of the term "peaceful rise" is partly due to your visit to the United States at the end of 2002, I somehow believe that it has much to do with your years in the Central Party School, when you attached importance to and constantly improved the course on "strategic mind-set." And even earlier than that you pointed out that when the third round of economic

globalization was getting under way in the early twenty-first century, we in China faced the dual missions of building an indus-
trialized and an information-based society, which presented dual
challenges and dual opportunities. You call this "three duals." The
concept was further highlighted in Jiang Zemin's political report
to the Sixteenth Party Congress, which noted that "an overview of
the situation shows that for our country the first two decades of
the twenty-first century are a period of important strategic
opportunities, which we must grasp firmly and which offer
bright prospects."

ZHENG: This is a good question. The emphasis on seizing
opportunities is an important feature of Deng Xiaoping's strategic thinking. Particularly in the late 1980s and early 1990s, he
kept stressing this point. He said that when an opportunity shows
up, we must seize it to speed up development. He also said he
was most concerned about missing opportunities.

YE: I remember that when you talked about seizing opportunities in the Party School, you also called for risk awareness. You
said that awareness and careful observation were needed because
of the many uncertainties, such as whether this round of economic globalization might again get out of control or even
worse, how serious the consequences of the growing gap between
North and South would be, the cold war mentality, various
threats to security, and all the difficulties on China's road to
domestic development.

ZHENG: Again, a good question. In Deng Xiaoping's strategic
thinking, "seizing opportunities" goes hand in hand with sober
assessment and improving capabilities to guard against and tol-

erate risks. Please note that the ability to tolerate risks as an important strategic concept was first put forward by Deng Xiaoping in May 1988 and was repeatedly stressed after that.

Having said that, the emphasis in Deng Xiaoping's strategic thinking was always on "seizing and not missing opportunities." Throughout the early 1990s, the importance of seizing opportunities, especially in the strategically important period of rare opportunities—the last decade of the twentieth century—was often brought up in his conversations with people from Shanghai, Jiangsu, and Zhejiang.

To mark the centenary of Deng Xiaoping's birth, the city of Shanghai and the Party Literature Research Center of the Central Committee of the Chinese Communist Party (CCP) made a long documentary entitled "Deng Xiaoping and Shanghai." One of the scenes shows how, after staying in Shanghai for Chinese New Year in 1994 (the last of seven Spring Festivals he spent there), when he was on the train about to leave and the step-board especially prepared for him had already been removed, he nevertheless asked Wu Bangguo and Huang Ju to get on board and talked with them for about ten minutes. Their conversation was mainly about how Shanghai should not miss opportunities, especially the last opportunities of the twentieth century. You are absolutely right that the key point of Deng Xiaoping's strategic thinking is seizing opportunities.

THE OVERALL INTERNATIONAL

AND DOMESTIC SITUATIONS

YE: Before the centenary of Deng Xiaoping's birth, you not only gave an exclusive interview to the *Guangming Daily*, but also wrote an article titled, "Memories of Compiling the *Selected*

Works of Deng Xiaoping (volume 3) under the Instruction of Comrade Deng Xiaoping." On both occasions, you mentioned Deng Xiaoping's strategic thoughts on the overall international and domestic situations. Why did you say that it was on the basis of this analysis that Deng Xiaoping had greatly deepened his strategic thought on seizing opportunities and his scientific understanding of socialism?

ZHENG: I said just now that one of the most important features of Deng Xiaoping's strategic thinking is to proceed from the overall domestic and international situations. In the summer of 1993, Deng Xiaoping did not go to Beidaihe, but personally took charge of compiling the *Selected Works of Deng Xiaoping* (volume 3). During this project, he said that, whether in the present or in the future, he spoke not from a narrow perspective but based on the overall situation.[3] These words are simple but profound. They fully reflect Deng Xiaoping's personal assessment of volume 3 of the *Selected Works*. At the same time, they represent his whole life experience as a great revolutionary leading his times. In our eyes, throughout his life, he had always observed things from an overall perspective. That is why, despite the dangers, vicissitudes, ups and downs of his life, he did not recoil in fear, shrink, or fall back; on the contrary, he forged ahead in a more profound and energetic way. This is what a great revolutionary should do. This is what the Deng Xiaoping spirit is all about; it is a very simple yet very profound and instructive summary of his spirit. Therefore, I believe that it also relates to Deng's Marxist political and theoretical courage. Only when one

61

3. July 7, 1993; see *Annals of Deng Xiaoping* (Beijing: Central Documents Publishing House), p. 1362.

truly grasps the overall situation can one have the political and theoretical courage he had. Otherwise, limited to a "narrow perspective," one would lose sight of the overall situation and then there would be no theoretical and political courage to talk about!

DENG XIAOPING SPECIALLY REQUIRED
THE WORD "STEADFAST" BE ADDED

YE: You said that the socialism with Chinese characteristics defined by Deng Xiaoping is a socialism that helps to constantly develop the productive forces and that favors peace. Now you have further touched upon Deng Xiaoping's strategic thoughts on the overall domestic and international situations. Could you further explain the relationship between these two lines of thought and their relationship to the development path of peaceful rise?

ZHENG: His thinking on the overall domestic and international situations forms the theoretical basis, while a socialism that helps to constantly develop the productive forces and favors peace—that is, socialism with Chinese characteristics—is the fundamental conclusion. In this way, we must take into account both international and domestic situations and both peace and development. That is to say, we should strive for a peaceful environment for our own development and in turn safeguard peace with our own development. This is the development path of peaceful rise. Deng Xiaoping said on his tour of inspection in South China, "China is a steadfast force for safeguarding world peace." I clearly remember that Deng Xiaoping specially highlighted the word *steadfast* when finalizing the draft of this speech.

YE: What are the challenges for China's peaceful rise?

ZHENG: In my opinion, we are confronted with three major challenges in the twenty-first century: resources, environment, and coordinated economic and social development. We face both new historical opportunities and three major challenges, which means that China is both in the prime time of its development and in a period of outstanding problems. This new historical juncture requires us to be sober minded and take proper measures. Since the Sixteenth Party Congress, both the Party Central Committee, with Jiang Zemin at the core, and the new central leadership, with Hu Jintao as general secretary, have been busy with this.

IF LINCOLN COULD DO IT, WHY CAN'T WE?

YE: There is also the question of Taiwan. Some say that conditions in today's world are unfavorable for China to realize its reunification through force, that nationalism is not the supreme principle any more, and that in wars and conflicts within a country, the traditional principle of noninterference by others no longer holds. What's your comment?

ZHENG: Besides the three major challenges I mentioned, there is indeed another huge risk and challenge: the Taiwan question. It is one of the points on China's new path of peaceful rise included in my speech at the thirtieth Villa d'Este Forum in Europe. I believe that China's development path of peaceful rise itself requires and facilitates peaceful reunification. The more developed China is, the more it will contribute to peaceful reunification. Therefore,

63

the CCP Central Committee has explicitly declared that as long as there is a glimmer of hope, no effort will be spared for peaceful reunification. However, if proponents of Taiwan's independence dare to go against the trend of history and split the country, or if foreign forces dare to interfere and support Taiwan's independence, we will never rule out the use of force. Even so, it will be a just action to protect the country against secession and to safeguard national unity, sovereignty, and territorial integrity. It is definitely not an act of invasion or expansion.

On this question, I told some American friends: look at your President Lincoln and see how firmly he maintained national unity and opposed secession. I quoted from Lincoln's inaugural speech on March 4, 1861, when he explicitly said, "In view of the Constitution and the laws, the Union is unbroken. . . . No State upon its own mere motion can lawfully get out of the Union." I also quoted from his famous letter written in August 1862, where he further stressed:

My paramount object in this struggle is to save the Union, and is not either to save or to destroy slavery. If I could save the Union without freeing any slave I would do it, and if I could save it by freeing all the slaves I would do it; and if I could save it by freeing some and leaving others alone I would also do that. What I do about slavery and the colored race, I do because I believe it helps to save the Union; and what I forbear, I forbear because I do not believe it would help to save the Union. I shall do less whenever I shall believe what I am doing hurts the cause, and I shall do more whenever I shall believe doing more will help the cause.

After quoting Lincoln's remarks, I told my American friends Lincoln's words and deeds at the moment were of critical importance. Otherwise, there wouldn't be an America today. Now, the question is why Lincoln's "paramount object" to save the Union is completely just, whereas the Chinese people cannot firmly safeguard our national unity?!

All in all, I believe that sovereignty and territorial integrity constitute the core interests of a country. This is an insurmountable principle and it will never be outdated.

YE: Now, I have a follow-up question. Do you think that proponents of Taiwan's independence are challenging China's peaceful rise?

ZHENG: That is correct. Those who support Taiwan's independence are the source of trouble. They not only undermine the prosperity and development of all of China, including Taiwan, but also compromise the tranquility of the Asia-Pacific region and the world at large. This is why we will never rule out the use of force against their secession activities. The concept of peaceful rise conforms entirely with firmly safeguarding national unity and territorial integrity and opposing secession.

65

NO SOVEREIGNTY AND SECURITY, NO PEACEFUL RISE

YE: Deng Xiaoping said, "State sovereignty and security should always be the top priority." However, advocates of Western liberal thought preach the universality of human rights. Their belief that there are legitimate, ethical reasons for intervention on the grounds of the protection of personal rights has directly led to various forms of "humanitarian intervention" in international affairs after the cold war. What's your comment on this?

ZHENG: There must be prerequisites and guarantees for peaceful rise. The most fundamental are state sovereignty and security.

Without state sovereignty and security, everything else would be out of the question. I believe that at present nation-states are the basic organizational units of the world and they will remain so for a long time to come. Although there are various international organizations, and despite economic globalization and regional integration, the partial integration of states, and even the partial transfer of sovereignty, the basic nation-state remains unchanged. It's even more true for China, given its national condition. Therefore, we must explicitly make state sovereignty and security the top priority. Only with this fundamental prerequisite and guarantee and in a peaceful international environment will it be possible for us to concentrate on development, on providing a good life for the 1.3 to 1.5 billion Chinese people. Of course, this will also be greatly beneficial to world peace and development.

Finally, I want to mention that in today's world, China is not the only country that seeks a peaceful rise. There are countries in the world marching toward peaceful rise with different approaches and models and at different paces. At the same time, the developed countries continue to grow. This is a major new trend in world peace and development. I think that, while realizing that the world is far from tranquil, we should fully acknowledge this major new trend in world peace and development and welcome it warmly.

A New Opportunity for Relations between China and the United States

Council on Foreign Relations, December 13, 2002

From Washington to New York, wherever I go in the States on my current trip, I hear a lot of American friends say that there is a new opportunity now for Chinese-U.S. relations. I very much echo their views, but the question is, how should we view this new opportunity for Chinese-U.S. relations?

Opportunity is an eternal theme. When Francis Bacon talked about opportunity he said, "Opportunity only favors those prepared minds." We may not be well prepared today to let opportunity favor us, but I believe we can at least talk about it.

In general, we talk about two types of opportunity for state-to-state relations. The first type is generated by changes in external factors and the second is determined by the development of inherent factors. As far as Chinese-U.S. relations are concerned, we have experienced the first type of opportunity. For example, for about one decade, from the 1970s to late 1980s, there existed a so-called big triangle strategic relationship between the United States, the U.S.S.R., and China. As a matter of fact, rivalry between the United States and the U.S.S.R. brought China and the United States together to cope with the Soviet threat, which in turn created an opportunity for Chinese-U.S. relations. I remember that during my first visit to the United States, in 1979, when we said the word *bear* at meetings with our American friends, everybody would know what we were talking about. That is because it instantly reminded us of the most important thing in common between the two states then; namely, dealing with that "polar bear." Since there was a polar bear out there threatening both of us, we became friends. So, a lot of credit should indeed be given to that bear.

However, in the 1990s, the U.S.S.R. disintegrated overnight. The sudden disappearance of the bear led people to wonder whether there still were opportunities for Chinese-U.S. relations. To some people in America, the bear took such opportunities with it. Thus, after that there were more troubles or even conflicts in the bilateral relationship.

It looks very much like a joke of destiny that the events of 9/11 seem to have brought back opportunities for Chinese-U.S. relations. As a result, when friends meet and talk about relations between our two countries, we hear the word *opportunity* again with some frequency. This leads me to think about what it is that constitutes the foundation of the opportunity, that can ensure that Chinese-U.S. relations will grow stably over the long term. Certainly, China and the United States share a position against terrorism. This is without any doubt important; thus, it is a new opportunity. But in view of what we have learned from our experience in the decade from the 1970s to the late 1980s and the subsequent twists and turns in the bilateral relationship, if some similar position against terrorism is the only thing that holds our two great nations together, isn't the relationship too fragile, even pathetic? Doesn't it make you feel sad? Do you believe that Chinese-U.S. relations could have sustained growth on the basis of that alone? Do you believe this could be the hope for the bilateral relationship?

Frankly, the opportunities generated by the big triangle, as we saw in the 1970s and the 1980s, and those brought by the events of 9/11 or some other hot issues are derived from outside factors. We cannot say such opportunities are not important, but if they are the only things we count on, we will fail to see the other side of the story. In particular, we will overlook the new circumstances of the twenty-first century, and the fact that China has been on the course of reform and development for twenty-three years and will continue on such a path.

I believe the biggest opportunity for Chinese-U.S. relations in the twenty-first century lies in China's development path, as far as the Chinese side is concerned (I do not intend to talk about the American side here). To support my argument, I would point to the following factors.

The first factor is the market. The Chinese market has huge potential, and this potential is being translated into purchasing power with increasing width and depth. The Chinese market is integrating with the world market more extensively and deeply. This trend will be a major phenomenon in the world economy in the twenty-first century. Doesn't this mean a big, sustained opportunity for the American economy, eager to tap into new markets? I do not need to give you any figures here.

The second factor is our system. Our system is not rigid, nor do we plan to make it so. A fundamental underpinning of our system is a market economy and the constant improvement of our democracy and political architecture.

It would take only one trip to China for you to discover how dynamic our economy is. Although it may appear a little chaotic, such economic dynamism comes from our market economy and gradual administrative and political deregulation. For example, our booming agricultural economy and the free flow of the rural labor force are directly related to the disbandment of people's communes. The major decision to close people's communes was made, publicly announced, and implemented by the Chinese Communist Party Central Committee in the 1980s. Now we have decided to reform China's state-owned enterprises with a share-holding system and have recognized that our share-holding system is a major instrument with which to invigorate public ownership of China. This, obviously, is another change. Might such a change herald important new opportunities for cooperation between China and the United States in various areas?

The third factor is culture. We also abide by a principle of opening up in making ideological and cultural progress. Cultural exchanges and cooperation between China and the United States constitute an important part of the development and growth of China's cultural industry. Let me take overseas students as an example. Hundreds of thousands of Chinese people have studied in the United States, more than in any other foreign country. One-fifth of them have already finished their studies and come back to China, and the remaining four-fifths are still in the United States, studying or working.

Don't these three factors, plus a lot of areas where both countries have common interests, mean a new, major, precious, and promising opportunity for Chinese-U.S. relations?

As you know, there is about U.S. $70 billion of American capital in the Chinese mainland, and more is expected in the future. Bilateral trade is also growing. America's huge information technology industry, IT talent pool, and numerous IT products—thanks to its achievement in the information revolution in the past decade—is well poised to enter China's booming information market. America's manufacturing industries and its service industries, including the financial and insurance sectors, will have a bigger and bigger presence in the China market. All in all, China's development, China's big development, China's sustained big development, is a major new opportunity for Chinese-U.S. relations. More important, this new opportunity has a sound foundation.

Given this, we can say that this new opportunity is rooted in, or is derived from, the development of inherent factors on the two sides, rather than any accidental outside factors. From this perspective, I think the opportunity for China and the United States to develop a constructive, cooperative relationship right now and in the future is much deeper, and thus much stronger, than the one we saw in the decade from the 1970s to 1980s, when we jointly fought the bear. Would you agree?

Let me emphasize one point here. Through more than two decades of reform and opening up, China has found a new path of development. This brand new path features developing in connection with economic globalization, instead of in isolation (let alone in confrontation with it), and building a socialism with Chinese characteristics . To elaborate, I think such a path needs to rely on our own development, market development and opening up, institutional innovation, structural adjustment, active participation in economic globalization, and relationships of mutual benefit and reciprocity with other countries. This is, indeed, a brand new path for China—a path of peaceful rise.

I believe that we can see more clearly from a long-term perspective that the biggest opportunity for Chinese-U.S. relations lies in the development of the two states. On the Chinese side, the biggest opportunity lies in China's path of peaceful rise in connection with economic globalization, which enables China to develop extensively and benefits other countries enormously as well.

Let's compare China's new path with what has happened in history. First of all, it is totally different from the path undertaken by any new power in modern history, for example, that pursued by Germany in World War I, or Germany and Japan in World War II, which wreaked such havoc with the world. Secondly, it is totally different from any path of rise in the history of socialism, such as the policies of the former U.S.S.R. under Brezhnev, which sought supremacy on the strength of a military bloc and an arms race.

Recall what Deng Xiaoping said on December 10, 1989, at a meeting with former president Bush's special envoy, Brent Scowcroft, when Chinese-U.S. relations were at a low point: "Chinese-U.S. relations have to be good." And he also said, "Mr. Envoy, please tell President Bush there is a retired old man in China who is solicitous about the improvement and growth of Chinese-U.S. relations." These remarks are very important and profound. They are not diplomatic parlance. Rather, they accurately captured the farsightedness of Deng Xiaoping's strategic thinking.

One of the reasons that I mention this episode here is that these words were spoken at a time when the ten-year-long opportunity for Chinese-U.S. relations had become troubled, thanks to the disappearance of some outside factors. Chinese-U.S. relations have now entered a new century and are facing a new opportunity. I believe this new opportunity can and should shift from relying on the whims of outside factors to relying on inherent factors, thus finding a more solid foundation.

So far, I have spoken from the perspective of China's development path. I have not talked about the American side, but this does not mean that there is no need to talk about it. I wish to say with all sincerity that it is up to both the Chinese and the American sides to fully understand, clearly expound, and firmly seize the new opportunities for Chinese-U.S. relations in the new century. Let me reiterate here that although circumstances have changed, we still need to remember Deng Xiaoping's profound words: "Chinese-U.S. relations have to be good."

THE SIXTEENTH NATIONAL CONGRESS OF THE CHINESE COMMUNIST PARTY AND CHINA'S PEACEFUL RISE: A NEW PATH

Center for Strategic and International Studies, December 9, 2002

I am delighted to meet with friends today. Let me start my presentation with some words about the leadership reshuffle at the Sixteenth National Congress of the Chinese Communist Party (CCP). The Sixteenth Party Congress was held at a key juncture, when the central leadership of the party as a whole needed to be reshuffled. The most significant outcome of the congress was that all the members—with the exception of Hu Jintao of the Standing Committee of the Political Bureau of the Central Committee of the CCP—were replaced with new faces. The most striking feature of the reshuffle was the smooth transition of power in an institutionalized manner. The Political Bureau of the CCP Central Committee, led by General Secretary Hu Jintao, was already up and running and the first meeting it called, which was covered in detail by the media on the same day, was about China's economic development and its people's living standard. Everyone in China is happy with the results of the Sixteenth Party Congress because it represents a new start and shows that the new leadership will do an even better job of upholding Deng Xiaoping's theory and the "three represents" and is giving top priority to development in its administration. At the same time, the smooth transition of power at the top levels of leadership is evidence that a new type of political culture has been born and is growing in China.

General Secretary Hu Jintao has rich experience working at the grass roots, and in particular in places with harsh conditions, such as Tibet, Guizhou Province, and Gansu Province. For ten years, he was a member of the Standing Committee of the Political Bureau of the CCP Central Committee. When he was concurrently president of the Central Party School, I was the executive vice president, so I had personal experience of his strong leadership and his support of teaching and academic reform at the school.

I would like to say a few words about teaching reform at the Central Party School. An important part of the reform is to fully understand contemporary world trends in economics, science, technology, law, and military affairs and thinking, in addition to in-depth study of the guiding principles of the CCP. We call this element "five contemporaries," and it means that cadres of the party at all levels should have a world-oriented outlook. I would welcome you all to the Central Party School, if you are interested and have the time; I would give you a more detailed introduction to our reforms. I would like you to know that our reform has got full backing from Hu Jintao. As he once said, "Cadres of the party at all levels should have a world-oriented outlook and shall by no means be out of touch with reality, stubborn or rigid." At the first press conference after he was appointed general secretary he said firmly and emphatically, "The main task for the new central leadership is to concentrate on development and growth."

Where is China heading in the twenty-first century? China has stuck to a path of development over the two decades since the Third Plenum of the Eleventh Party Congress. Thanks to this, gross domestic product (GDP) grew 7.4-fold from 1980 to 2001, at an average annual growth rate of 9.5 percent, which has improved living standards for the Chinese people as a whole.

The Sixteenth Party Congress decided to quadruple China's GDP by 2020; that is, to raise it from U.S. $1 trillion in 2000 to U.S. $4 trillion through two decades of hard work. Per capita GDP will grow from U.S. $800 in 2000 to U.S. $3,000 in 2020. This decision will be submitted as a new development target to the National People's Congress. The CCP Central Committee also explicitly said that even when this target is met, it will only bring China into the fold of low-end, medium-level developed nations and there will still be a lot of difficulties and problems on the road ahead.

What are these problems? I think the biggest economic problem China has is the dual structure in its urban and rural areas. When you travel to China, you find some prosperous big cities. But if you go to the rural areas, you will notice a huge gap with the cities, not only in the western regions, but also in the central and even the eastern parts of the country. This represents the biggest problem. On top of that, a large number of workers got laid off due to unbalanced industrial development. Thus, the CCP Central Committee believes that we need to dedicate the first twenty years of the twenty-first century to quadrupling China's GDP and building a well-off society all round. This means that we need to be prudent instead of complacent, and that we must not get carried away by the new circumstances of the new century. This represents where China is and what China can begin with. On the other hand, this is a grand blueprint the party has drawn up. This alone is ambitious enough to engross the whole nation, from the leadership down to ordinary people, for two decades.

25

What, then, does building a well-off society in an all-round fashion mean? I believe the first component of this goal is to achieve comprehensive growth in the national economy, so as to alleviate a series of key challenges, including the disparity between cities and rural areas in different parts of the country, and the need to adjust the industrial structure and gradually let "informatization" drive industrialization. Let me share some figures about the development of information technology in China.

By the end of August of this year, China will have 180 million mobile phone subscribers, more than any other country in the world, including the United States. If we put mobile and fixed-line service together, the total number will reach 380 million. In 1990, a mere twelve years ago, very few people in China had mobile phones, and thus they were viewed as a luxury. Moreover, over 43 million people in China spend more than one hour per day online, putting China third in the world—and this number is growing fast. I am not trying to show off what China has achieved. Instead, I want to highlight that China's growth rate is not low, although as a nation of 1.3 billion people, we have a lot more to catch up with.

The second component of our goal is to achieve balance in our material, political, and spiritual cultures. I would like to call your attention to the fact the Sixteenth Party Congress, for the first time ever, decided to build a socialist political culture. The simple interpretation of "political culture" is democracy plus the rule of law; namely, the building of socialist democratic politics and a country ruled by law. This target has multiple dimensions, including political culture as demonstrated by the smooth hand-over of power at top levels of leadership and direct elections at the grassroots level in the rural areas. We have a lot to accomplish to build a socialist political culture, and we need to overcome a lot of problems and challenges. However, having this framework target of building a political culture is totally different from not having it.

The third component is to achieve all-round human development. Fundamentally, this means paying more attention to and trying hard to meet the various needs of the people. The progress of informatization in terms of the number of mobile phone users, fixed-line users, web users, and mobile phone free-move is, I believe, part of development for ordinary people. Another example is education. Without an increase in the penetration of education, and the provision of better education, there is nothing whatsoever of all-round human development to talk about. The penetration rate of ordinary education in China has risen from 30 percent twenty years ago to above 90 percent. The illiteracy rate among young people has fallen to 5 percent. The area of housing per capita in the cities is twenty-one square meters and in the rural areas it is even more, so it is fair to say that housing conditions are also improving. Let's think about this. If residents in one country do not have basic housing, do not have adequate access to education or information, how can all-round development for all be possible?

Once again, I am not boasting about how well China is currently doing. My point is that, with 1.3 billion people in mind, the CCP is working hard to meet the demands of the variety of ordinary people's needs, such as clothing, food, housing, transportation, and daily necessities. Without this, there would not be a "well-off society in an all-round way."

The Sixteenth Party Congress adopted a series of principles so as to meet the new development targets. Here, I would like to focus on two of them.

The first principle concerns domestic policy. At the Sixteenth Congress, it was decided to mobilize all positive factors in the most extensive and adequate manner for the great rejuvenation of the Chinese nation. One thing new implied here is the emphasis on side-by-side development of all economic elements. About ten years ago, the nonpublic sector in China contributed less than 1 percent to GDP. This figure has risen to 43 percent. The output of the self-employed and private enterprises is 117 times that of the early 1990s, and their number has grown 19.5-fold. The number of people working in those nonpublic sectors has grown by 54 million. China now has more than 25 million self-employed individuals and more than 1.7 million private enterprises. The Sixteenth Party Congress stressed that China would give full play to different economic components and encourage the growth of the self-employed and private economies. The CCP Charter was revised at the Sixteenth Party Congress to explicitly state that members of the private and self-employed sectors can join the party if they are qualified.

The second principle concerns China's foreign cooperation. To put it simply, this means to continue to expand its opening up. Put differently, it means to be in tandem with economic globalization, instead of isolating itself. China has been reforming and opening up for more than two decades. With an inflow of more than U.S. $50 billion in 2002, it may be that China attracts more foreign capital than the United States. Wal-Mart, AIA, and Citibank all have a presence in China, and the Chinese people are gradually accepting these foreign names. Britain's Standard Life and some big Japanese insurance companies have been given the go-ahead by the China Insurance Regulatory Commission (CIRC). Foreign banks will start their RMB business in five cities in China, including Shanghai, Shenzhen, Guangzhou, and Zhuhai, from December 5 of this year.

In summary, to implement the blueprint that the CCP has drawn for the new century, we need to have a new path of development. China's path will be totally different from those of all the major powers in the modern world. This will be a brand new path of development.

I want to emphasize one point here. Our path is different from the paths both of Germany in World War I and of Germany and Japan in World War II, when they tried to overhaul the world political landscape by means of aggressive wars. Our path is also different from that of the former U.S.S.R. under President Brezhnev, which relied on a military bloc and an arms race in order to compete with the United States for world supremacy.

Our brand new path relies upon the following factors: our own development; the opening up of markets; institutional innovation; connection with economic globalization instead of being isolated; and reciprocity and mutually beneficial relationships with other countries.

In truth, this new path of China's peaceful rise was not invented today. We have been on this track for twenty-three years, and we have benefited enormously from it. So why should we change it? I wish to frankly tell you one more thing. The Chinese Communist Party, following the Sixteenth Party Congress, has made up its mind to stay on the path of peaceful rise, to achieve peaceful rise through a long period of hard work in the twenty-first century.

How should we view where China is heading in the twenty-first century, and how should we view China's development path? I leave these questions with you, as your homework for today. To think about them, I believe you will need a change of mind-set. Our reform and opening up over the past two decades is a result of a changed mind-set. Don't you also need to change your mindset, at least a little bit? I propose that we change our mind-sets together. Will you all come on board?

CHINA'S TWO HISTORIC PURSUITS IN MODERN TIMES

John F. Kennedy School of Government, Harvard University,
December 4, 1997

It is a great pleasure for me to share with you some of my thoughts about where China is heading at the turn of the century. This is such a big topic, so I wish to focus my presentation on one crucial point, namely, that at the turn of the century, the world-oriented, future-oriented, and modernization-oriented reform and opening up of China is irreversible. The Chinese leadership is deeply committed to a peaceful path of development after carefully sizing up the situation, pondering on this issue, and prudently choosing from the different options.

I believe I can be very frank with the dear friends present today. I am not trying to be diplomatic; rather, I firmly believe what I am saying. The choice of such a development path is a decision of fundamental significance, not a matter of expediency. It is not an impulsive decision; rather, it is deeply grounded in what we have learned from the past.

The Chinese nation's aspiration for modernization is one and a half centuries old, starting approximately from Lin Zexu in the 1840s. You may know that he led the famous campaign to ban opium in China, but you probably do not know that he was also "the first in modern Chinese history to open his eyes to the world," meaning that he was the first to seriously think about emulating the Western industrial revolution in China. Five generations since Lin Zexu have pursued and strived for modernization; nevertheless, modernization has yet to become a reality in China.

The Chinese nation has been subject to too much suffering. People all remember vividly that China's embrace of the twentieth century was marked by foreign allied forces' occupation of the capital city, Beijing, in 1900. As a Sichuan native, I remember my father once told me that when they heard, far away from the capital in Southwest Sichuan, about the Eight Allied Forces' occupation of Beijing, they all burst into tears. Deep in their hearts, the people all felt so humiliated. As a result, the pursuit of state sovereignty and territorial integrity, on the one hand, and development and modernization, on the other hand, have been the deepest drives and the loftiest ideals for successive generations of Chinese over the past 150 years.

You can say that Sun Yat-sen, Mao Zedong, and Deng Xiaoping represent the three historic transformations that the Chinese nation has undergone in the last century, and the pursuit of state sovereignty and territorial integrity, and development and modernization were an integral part of all three transformations. Why do the Chinese people remember Sun Yat-sen? Because he, along with his colleagues, overthrew the monarchy and founded a republic. Why do the Chinese people remember Mao Zedong? Because under the leadership of Mao and the Chinese Communist Party (CCP), the Chinese nation rose to its legitimate position among nations of the world. Why do the Chinese people remember Deng Xiaoping? Because by initiating reform and opening up, he and the Communist Party put China for the first time ever on the path toward modernization in conjunction with instead of in isolation from economic globalization, and as a result, China has been fundamentally transformed.

Of course, the Chinese leadership is fully aware both of the enormous opportunities and of the huge challenges and risks we face at the turn of the century. First of all, with 1.2 billion people, China is endowed with a vast market and a huge pool of talent, but a big population gives rise to many difficult challenges, such as employment and food. We should be mindful of the fact that China's population is still growing and will peak at 1.5 billion in 2020 or 2030. One can say that any reform and opening up we do today is, to some degree, to brace for the population peak. Second, amid our innovative efforts to build a socialist market economy, we need to work long and hard to resolve difficult issues such as how public ownership fits with a market economy, how the public sector can compete effectively in the market, and how we can integrate with economic globalization without being vulnerable to all its associated risks. Third, while we freely draw on these high points of other world civilizations, we are nevertheless exposed to bad influences from their decadent aspects. Fourth, as an ancient civilization in the East, thousands of years old, China is blessed with fine traditions. However, we are also burdened with bad legacies of the past. Fifth, we have run into massive and multidimensional ecological, environmental, and social problems in the process of industrialization.

I remember President Franklin Roosevelt once said, sixty years ago when he was trying to promote the New Deal, "We hear so many voices when we are faced with a major decision." It happened to you and it is the same for us. People have different views and opinions in the face of challenges and risks, and this has drawn the attention of the international community, including experts and scholars present today. The various debates about the so-called post-Deng era that we all heard so often some time ago are a case in point. Now the dust has settled, with the explicit statement of the CCP at its Fifteenth Party Congress, where General-Secretary Jiang Zemin solemnly pledged the whole party to unswervingly uphold the great banner of Deng Xiaoping's thoughts and move ahead the great cause of building socialism with Chinese characteristics in an all-round fashion toward the twenty-first century. This was also written into the charter of CCP—the cardinal document guiding the party. In fact, efforts to reform and open up intensified after this, because it represents what the people want and nothing can turn it back.

I think friends may also note that the past two decades, from the Third Plenum of the Eleventh Party Congress through the Twelfth, Thirteenth, Fourteenth, and Fifteenth Party Congresses, have not been smooth sailing. The other side of the coin, which I believe also warrants more attention, is that despite ups and downs, China did not get turned away from the path of reform, opening up, and socialist modernization, and indeed efforts toward these ends demonstrated stronger and stronger momentum as time elapsed. This leads us to the conclusion that any endeavor in China can be promising and full of life only when it coincides with the nation's pursuit of, first, state sovereignty and territorial integrity, and second, development and modernization. Otherwise, it will be doomed to failure and oblivion.

I have three points to make about the impact that China's drive to reform, opening up, and modernization might have on the world. First of all, China's stability is, in itself, a contribution to the world. Deng Xiaoping repeatedly said that if China, a country of 1.2 billion people, fails to remain stable, and as a result refugees, not in their millions or tens of millions but in hundreds of millions, flee the country, it would cause a global catastrophe. Any responsible political leader must take this very seriously. Hence, the drive to combine reform, development, and stability shows how responsible China is toward the rest of the world and mankind as a whole.

Second, China's reform and development is a contribution, too. The number of people in poverty in China has dropped from 250 million at the end of the 1970s to 50 million in 1997 and to 20 million at the end of this century. Isn't this a contribution to mankind? As reform and development progress, China not only is able to supply more commodities to the world, but also can provide the world with a bigger market. In the remaining years of this century, China needs, for example to increase its electricity capacity by 80 million kilowatts, railway mileage by 16,000 kilometers, expressway mileage by 28,000 kilometers, fiber optic cable by 150,000 kilometers, and telephone exchange control equipment by 80 million. China's foreign trade will reach U.S. $400 billion in 2000. China will undoubtedly become an even bigger market in the first decade of the next century. This will contribute to the prosperity not only of China but also of all the nations competing in the Chinese market.

Third, China needs a peaceful international environment and will contribute to it. During his tour of South China in 1992, Deng Xiaoping famously said, "China is a staunch force safeguarding world peace."

We can see from the above that world peace and development offers very good opportunity for China, and China's reform and development provides a very good opportunity for the whole world (including the United States). This signals a tremendous and profound convergence of strategic interests that overcomes differences of ideology and social regime.

China was not the originator of the cold war mentality; rather, we were a victim of it. Therefore China hopes all the more to lay to rest this way of thinking incompatible with contemporary times. Generations of Chinese were subject to threat and humiliation by foreign powers, so China is opposed to other countries threatening us and is less inclined to threaten others. China lagged behind and was humiliated because we failed to jump on the bandwagon of the European and American industrial revolutions. China's arrogance in the past, when it looked down upon foreign countries as "barbarians," was mocked and penalized by history. Some Western people have been quick to finger-point China as a threat when they see any slight improvement in the living standard of the Chinese, simply because they have been so used to seeing China poor and weak and cannot come to terms with its rejuvenation. Isn't this another type of arrogance, at odds with the times and deserving careful scrutiny and reflection?

Allow me to digress for a few moments. China and the United States, after all, have had such different experiences and their circumstances are different. If we all recognize this, it may be possible to understand why Darwin's "survival of the fittest" theory, as expressed in T. H. Huxley's *Evolution and Ethics,* was the first work of Western philosophy to shake up the Chinese intelligentsia in the post–Lin Zexu era. We realized that if we lagged behind, we would not survive; instead, we would be weeded out. (I believe this never occurred to either Huxley or Darwin at the time.) I would draw your attention to one more thing. In the mid-1950s, well after the People's Republic of China was founded, Mao Zedong said something to this effect: if China is content with being left behind, we will not have a foothold on the planet. We rarely see so profound a sense of crisis in the political and philosophical history of the United States.

Having said this, I would further impress upon you the fact that the Chinese people have been beset by a profound sense of crisis for generations. We have all along been thinking about how to guarantee our nation's survival and our rights to development, how to protect state sovereignty and territorial integrity and achieve development and modernization instead of ongoing expansion or invasion. The Chinese people today feel most fortunate to have found a peaceful path of development to build a prosperous, democratic, and cultivated socialist country with Chinese characteristics. We are most proud of that. Nevertheless, in view of challenges and risks in front of us, we have no reason to feel complacent.

I wish to conclude by quoting from Deng Xiaoping, who said, "We need to be sober-minded, sober-minded, and sober-minded, and make concrete efforts to do well what we need to do on our own and what we are doing." He also said, "With stable policies of reform and opening up, China has great promise." This fundamental principle has taken root among ordinary Chinese people. Indeed, it epitomizes where China is heading at the turn of the century, or even beyond.

CHINA'S PEACEFUL RISE

Speeches of Zheng Bijian, 1997–2005

C HINA'S rapid development has been a striking feature of the international landscape in recent years. In this timely collection, Zheng Bijian, one of China's leading thinkers and writers on ideological questions, addresses how we should think about China now.

His message is, first and foremost, that China hopes to rise not through territorial expansion or challenges to other powers but as a result of its own hard work and a peaceful international environment. The internal challenges are many: resource shortages, pollution, corruption, the need for a rule of law, and uneven socioeconomic development. Internationally, China faces a host of established powers—most notably the United States—with their own economic and political concerns. Zheng believes that clearly explaining his country's intentions can help establish the basis of a larger cooperative framework that will smooth China's growth in economic and political influence. With wit and insight, drawing on Abraham Lincoln, Franklin Roosevelt, and T. H. Huxley, as well as world history and China's own experiences, Zheng builds a picture of the political and policy constraints and opportunities in relations with China.

ABOUT THE AUTHOR

ZHENG BIJIAN is chairman of the China Reform Forum, a Beijing-based think tank working on domestic and international issues. He was formerly executive vice president of the Central Party School, serving as deputy to Chinese President Hu Jintao.

BROOKINGS INSTITUTION PRESS
Washington, D.C.
www.brookings.edu

ISBN 0-8157-9725-7

9 780815 797258

90000>